How Compatible Are You?

Your Relationship Quiz Book

Allan & Barbara Pease

How Compatible Are You?

Your Relationship Quiz Book

Pease International

Copyright © Allan Pease 2004

First published in Australia in 2004 by Pease International Pty Ltd
PO Box 1260, Buderim, QLD 4556, Australia.
Tel: + 61 7 5445 5600   Fax: + 61 7 5445 5688

Distributed in the United Kingdom by Pease International UK
Liberty House, 16 Newbold Terrace, Leamington Spa, CV32 4EG, United Kingdom
Tel: + 44 (0) 1926 88 99 00   Fax: + 44 (0) 1926 42 11 00

Distributed in Australia & New Zealand by HarperCollins Publishers
Distributed in Singapore by STP Books
Distributed in South Africa by Oxford University Press
Distributed in Hong Kong by Publishers Associates Ltd

All rights reserved. Apart from any use permitted under Australian copyright law,
this publication may only be reproduced, stored, or transmitted, in any form, or by
any means, with prior permission in writing of the publishers or, in the case of
reprographic production, in accordance with the terms of licences issued by the
Copyright Licensing Agency.

National Library of Australia
Cataloguing-in-publication data

ISBN: 192081609-7

Typeset by Bookhouse, Sydney
Printed in Australia by McPhersons Printing

Every effort has been made to fulfil requirements with regard to reproducing
copyright material. The author and publisher will be glad to rectify any omissions
at the earliest opportunity.

www.peaseinternational.com

Introduction

The misunderstandings and the conflict between the sexes, even in the twenty-first century, are still as real in our lives as they were when Adam first fell foul of Eve. During three decades of research into the differences between men and women, Barbara and I have been asked thousands of questions about why men and women behave in certain ways. The letters, the phone calls and the emails come from people mystified by the kind of things the opposite sex does, and from those who feel frustrated or helpless when it comes to knowing exactly how to deal with them. As a result of our research and the great interest shown in the differences between the way men and women think and act, we wrote the two bestselling books *Why Men Don't Listen and Women Can't Read Maps* and *Why Men Don't Have A Clue & Women Always Need More Shoes* to help people better understand and communicate with each other.

This new quiz book now gives you the opportunity to put yourself and your partner to the test concerning these many questions. We developed these special quizzes based on the most important chapters of our previous books and what we know will help you understand how you and your partner think.

What does your partner really know about you? Does your partner listen to you when you speak? Does your partner have better spatial abilities than you do? And how about driving and parking – who is better? What type of partner suits you best? Are you a good lover? Is your friendship ready to become a relationship? Is he or she likely to be faithful? Is the crisis in your relationship really the fault of your mother-in-law? Or are you responsible? Does your partner lie to you? Do you and your partner talk at cross-purposes?

These and many more questions can now be answered. The quizzes in this book will reveal new and exciting things about you and your partner. And you can start right now!

Have fun with this quiz book!

Allan & Barbara Pease

Contents

Introduction

Chapter 1
Talking and Listening

Why Men Don't Talk Much And Women Talk A Lot............3
The Basics of Listening 4
The Great Listening Test 5
Evaluate Your Need to Talk 10
Evaluations 15

Chapter 2
Spatial Ability

Knowing What's What and Where's Where 23
Test Your Spatial Skills 25
Test Your Ability to Read Maps and Your
    Navigational Skills... 28
Solutions 37
Test Evaluation 43
Can You Improve Your Spatial Skills? 44
Alternative Strategies 45

Chapter 3
Parking and Driving

Each According to Their Own	49
At First Sight	50
The Great Test of Driving and Parking	51
Evaluations	64

Chapter 4
The Opposite Sex

How to Find the Right Partner	69
The Ideal Partner	71
Is Your Relationship Intact?	74
The Great Romance Test	76
Evaluations	81
How to Make Romance Run Smoothly	84

Chapter 5
Marriage, Love, Romance & Sex

One Man – One Woman	91
Sex Does Not Equal Sex	92
Are You Ready For Marriage?	94
The Unmasking of Faithfulness	96
Are You Resistant to Pressure?	101
Evaluations	104

Chapter 6
Truth Will Out

Types of Lies	111
Who Lies the Most?	113
The Little Test of Swindles and White Lies	115
The Ultimate Lie Detector Test	118
Evaluations	129

Chapter 7
The Other Woman – His Mother

Enter the Dragon 135
Warming Yourself Up 136
The Great Endurance Test 138
The Ultimate Mother-in-Law Test 140
Mother and Daughter-in-Law –
    How Well Do They Get Along? 147
Evaluations 149

Chapter 8
Language Problems

Basic Rules of Communication 159
The Great Test of Communication 161
The Art of Giving the Right Answer 168
What's That Supposed to Mean? – The Enlightening Test..175
Evaluations 180

Why not use Allan Pease as guest speaker for your next conference or seminar?

Pease International (Australia) Pty Ltd
Pease International (UK) Ltd

P.O. Box 1260
Buderim 4556
Queensland
AUSTRALIA
Tel: ++61 7 5445 5600
Fax: ++61 7 5445 5688

Liberty House
16 Newbold Terrace
Leamington Spa CV 32 4 EG
UNITED KINGDOM
Tel: ++44 (0)1926 889900
Fax: ++44 (0)1926 421100

email: (Aust) info@peaseinternational.com
(UK) ukoffice@peaseinternational.com
website: www.peaseinternational.com

Also by Allan Pease:

Video Programs
- Body Language Series
- Silent Signals
- The Interview
- How to Make Appointments by Telephone

DVD Programs
- The Best of Body Language
- How to Develop Powerful Communication—Managing the Differences Between Men and Women

Audio Programs
- The Four Personality Styles
- How to Make Appointments by Telephone
- How to Remember Names, Faces & Lists
- Why Men Don't Listen and Women Can't Read Maps
- Questions are the Answers

Books
- The Definitive Book Of Body Language
- Why Men Don't Listen & Women Can't Read Maps
- Why Men Lie & Women Cry
- Why Men Can Only Do One Thing At A Time & Women Never Stop Talking
- How Compatible Are You?
- Talk Language
- Write Language
- Questions Are The Answers
- The Bumper Book of Rude & Politically Incorrect Jokes
- Politically Incorrect Jokes Men Love

How Compatible Are You?

Your Relationship Quiz Book

Chapter 1

Talking and Listening

What Males Hear vs What Females Say

What females say – what males hear

Why Men Don't Talk Much and Women Talk a Lot

We've known for thousands of years that men aren't great conversationalists, particularly when compared to women. Speech is not a major brain skill of men as it is with women. It operates mainly in a male's left brain and has no specific locations. MRI scans show that when a male speaks, the entire left hemisphere of his brain becomes active as it searches to find a centre for speaking.

Men evolved as lunch-chasers, not communicators. The hunt was conducted with a series of body language signals and often the hunters would sit for hours silently watching for their prey. They didn't talk or bond. When modern men go fishing together, they can sit for hours and say little to nothing. They're having a great time enjoying each other's company, but they don't feel the need to express it in words. Yet if women were spending time together and not talking, it would be indicative of a major problem.

In women, speech is a specific area located primarily in the front left hemisphere, and in other smaller, specific areas in

the right hemisphere. Having speech centres in both sides of the brain makes women good conversationalists. Because they have larger, specific areas that control speech, the rest of a woman's brain is available for other tasks, thus enabling her to do a number of different things at the same time. Women's clear-cut speech centres give them superiority of language and verbal dexterity.

Since women originally spent their days together with the other women and children in a group, they developed the ability to communicate successfully to maintain relationships.

The Basics of Listening

Typically, a woman can use an average of six listening expressions in a ten-second period to reflect, then, feed back the speaker's emotions. A woman reads the meaning of what is being said through voice intonation and the speaker's body language. This is exactly what a man needs to be able to do to capture a woman's attention – and keep her listening. Most men are daunted by the prospect of using facial feedback while listening, but it pays big dividends for the man who becomes proficient at it.

The biological objective of our ancestral male warrior when listening was to remain impassive, so as not to betray his emotions. This emotionless mask that men use while listening allows them to feel in control of the situation. It does not mean he isn't experiencing emotions; brain scans reveal that men feel emotion as strongly as women, but avoid showing it.

 # The Great Listening Test

The following questions can put your partner to the listening test. He or she can't fool you easily. Do they really listen to you or not? Do they really know your special likes and dislikes, or do they only pretend to? And what about you? Do you frequently expect too much of your partner and his speech ability or can you deal with his weaknesses? This quiz will bring the truth into the open.

If you are a man, take the test on page 8. Women should fill in the questions on *the next* page. If you want to test yourselves the other way round as well, make sure you copy the questionnaires before completing them.

Answer the questions carefully and ask your partner to fill in his/her answers afterwards – without having read your answers.

Your name _____

1. What upset you most this past week?

   _____

2. As a child, did you have a pet? If yes, what was it?

   _____

3. What happened in your last dream?

   _____

4. Which film moved you most during the past weeks or months, and why?

   _____

5. When is your best friend's birthday?

   _____

6. Do you believe in an after-life?

   _____

7. Which of your partner's habits annoys you most?

   _____

8. How can your partner always make you happy?

   _____

9. Which book are you reading or have you finished recently?

   _____

10. Do you feel that your partner listens to you?

    _____

11. Are you and your problems in good hands with your partner?

    _____

12. Do you idolise anyone? If yes, who is it?

    _____

13. To which country would you most like to travel?

    _____

14. What New Year resolutions did you make last year?

    _____

15. Do you have principles? Name the three most important.

    _____

    _____

Your Partner's Test

Your name _____

1. What upset your partner most this past week?

   ....

2. As a child, did your partner have a pet? If yes, what was it?

   ....

3. What happened in your partner's last dream?

   ....

4. Which film moved your partner most during the past weeks or months? And why?

   ....

5. When is your partner's best friend's birthday?

   ....

6. Does your partner believe in an after-life?

   ....

7. Which of your habits annoys your partner most?

   ....

8. How can you always make your partner happy?

   ....

9. Which book is your partner reading or has he/she finished recently?

   ....

10. Does your partner feel that you listen to him/her?

    ....

11. Does your partner think that he/she and his/her problems are in good hands with you?

    ....

12. Does your partner idolise anyone? If yes, who is it?

    ....

13. To which country would your partner most like to travel?

    ....

14. Which New Year resolutions did your partner make last year?

    ....

15. Does your partner have principles? Name their three most important.

    ....

    ....

Evaluate Your Need to Talk

The building of relationships through talking is a priority in the brain-wiring of women. A woman can effortlessly speak an average of 6,000 – 8,000 words a day. She uses an additional 2,000 – 3,000 sounds, vocally, to communicate, as well as 8,000 – 10,000 gestures, facial expressions, head movements and other body language signals. This gives her a daily maximum of over 20,000 communication 'units' to relate her messages.

Contrast a woman's daily 'chatter' to that of a man. He utters just 2,000 – 4,000 words and 1,000 – 2,000 vocal sounds, and makes a mere 2,000 – 3,000 body language signals. His daily average adds up to around 7,000 communication 'units' – about one third of the output of a woman.

How would you estimate your personal need to talk? Would you describe it as high or low? And does that correspond to the latest results of talk research? In the questions below, tick the answers that you most agree with and you will find out. There are no right or wrong answers and the points allocated do not reflect 'good' or 'bad' results.

1. **You are on a hiking tour with your partner. After four hours of ascent you reach the summit. What do you do?**
   a) You enjoy the view in silence and think to yourself that it was worth the effort. (0 points)
   b) You walk around a bit, take a good look at everything and then remark on the fantastic view. (3 points)
   c) Because your partner is not standing close to you, you call someone on your mobile to tell them about the fantastic view. If you can't reach anybody you send a text-message. After all, you have to share your feeling of happiness with someone. (5 points)

2. **You have a fondness for origami and are trying an extremely tricky model when your partner comes in and wants to tell you something. How do you react?**
   a) No problem. You continue to work while listening to your partner. (5 points)
   b) You feel disturbed in your concentration and ask your partner to come back a bit later as you are nearly finished and do not want to interrupt your work right now. (0 points)
   c) You make a break and talk to him/her. (3 points)

3. **You think fishing is ...**
   a) Wonderful! A useful activity where you don't have to talk and can think without interference for a while – even if you are with a whole group of people. (0 points)
   b) Absolutely boring. You don't understand what fun there might be in sitting the whole day by a lake in deep silence, waiting for a fish to bite. (5 points)
   c) It's OK from time to time. Especially when you feel like you need rest and relaxation. But you could just as easily go to the movies with friends. (3 points)

4. **How do you behave while solving a difficult mathematical task?**
   a) You mumble or talk to yourself all the time because this makes it easier for you to solve the problem. (5 points)
   b) You focus on the problem in silence and concentrate fully on the solution. You hardly sense the world around you. (0 points)
   c) You try for a while to figure it out. If you can't find the solution yourself you ask somebody for help. (3 points)

5. **Do you find it unpleasant to be sitting with a group of people and to experience long periods of silence during the conversation?**
   a) No. (0 points)
   b) That depends on the situation. Sometimes it can be wonderful, sometimes extremely depressing. (3 points)
   c) Yes, because you always think something might be wrong. (5 points)

6. Your boss offers you a new field of work. You ask him for an hour to think about it and you:
   a) immediately call your partner to discuss all the pros and cons. Perhaps you also talk to some of your colleagues if you are still uncertain. (5 points)
   b) carefully think about the opportunity and ask somebody for advice, if you are stuck. (3 points)
   c) switch on your answering machine, close the door to your office and ask your colleagues not to disturb you for the next hour. Then you ponder the offer and weigh all possibilities carefully. (0 points)

7. When you are watching an exciting film on TV, you:
   a) watch spellbound but don't have a problem with taking a brief phone call or having another conversation. (3 points)
   b) concentrate fully on the film. You neither answer the phone nor talk to anybody, nor do you do any other tasks because you can't follow the plot properly and will be annoyed afterwards. (0 points)
   c) might read the paper, do various other tasks, make phone calls or talk to somebody and still be able to follow the film's plot perfectly well. (5 points)

8. What do you consider is the point of talking?
   a) It's essential in forming relationships and maintaining friendships. (5 points)
   b) It's mainly to convey facts and information. (0 points)
   c) That depends on the circumstances, but basically both of the aspects mentioned above. (3 points)

9. If something bothers you, you will ...
   a) have to talk to somebody about it immediately, because otherwise the problem haunts you the whole day and you can't think of anything else. (5 points)
   b) It depends on how much else you have to do and how serious the problem is. You either try to solve it on your own or you confide in somebody. (3 points)
   c) You can easily put the matter out of your mind for some time until you can or want to think further about it. (0 points)

10. You are at your favourite Italian restaurant with your partner. Most of the evening is passed in silence. What do you think?
   a) Depends on whether there was any disagreement beforehand. Sometimes you rather enjoy being silent together. (3 points)
   b) Nothing much. You enjoy the food and your partner's company and give yourself up to your own thoughts. (0 points)
   c) You're wondering whether your partner is angry with you or doesn't love you any more. (5 points)

Evaluations

The Great Listening Test

Compare your answers to those of your partner and note how often they are...
 a) matching
 b) similar
 c) contrary

For identical answers you get 5 points, for similar answers 3 points and for contrary answers 0 points. Any unanswered questions are rated with 0 points.

> Number of matching answers × 5 points = ___
> Number of similar answers × 3 points = ___
> Number of contrary answers × 0 points = ___ (0)
> Total score = ___

75 to 65 Points

You have an outstanding relationship. Your points show that you and your partner can not only talk but also listen well to each other. Good communication is the best basis for a longstanding relationship.

64 to 45 Points

You do have the occasional problem in your communication but basically you have found a good way of talking and

listening to each other. If both of you are content with your present state of affairs you don't have to change anything. Alternatively you could try and find a way to improve the situation.

Less than 45 Points Points

Communication between you and your partner is not the best. You either have not known each other for long and have not become very familiar with each other yet or you should (re)read our first book *Why Men Don't Listen And Women Can't Read Maps* as soon as possible. It will teach you how to communicate effectively with your partner.

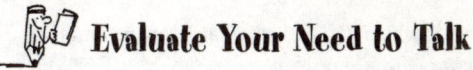 Evaluate Your Need to Talk

Add your points and read the corresponding section below.

50 to 40 Points

You are most likely a woman or a gay man, because your need to talk is great. Often, even at the end of a long day you have not fulfilled your daily quota of communication 'words' and therefore still have a lot to talk about. That's great if your partner feels the same way. If not, you should be careful not to expect too much of him and thus make him angry. When you begin speaking your unused words, he'll wonder why you won't be quiet and leave him in peace. He feels like he's been 'nagged to death'! "All I want is a bit of peace and quiet!" he thinks. Show a little consideration. He's a hunter, remember. He's been chasing lunch all day. He just wants to gaze into the fire. But this doesn't mean that he's not interested in you or that something's wrong.

39 to 15 Points

You are either a woman with a lower need to talk or a man who likes to talk more than most other men. Your need to talk

is determined by your whole day and by what happened around you and this can vary from day to day.

As long as you can convey this to your partner and he or she knows how to handle it, it will be positive for your relationship.

In a relationship, partners need to discuss their different ways of communicating. Men need to understand that when a woman talks, she is not expecting him to respond with solutions; nor is she trying to drive him crazy by giving him all the details of what she intends to do that day. Women need to understand that when a man doesn't talk, that is not a cue for believing something is wrong.

Less Than 15 Points

You are most likely a man, because your need to talk is low. You don't want to talk about everything and everyone but value moments of peace and silence when you don't have to think about anything.

It would be wonderful if your partner thought the same way, but women in general enjoy talking often and much more. It's wired into the female brain to talk and to use speech as a main form of expression, so don't hold it against her – this is one of her strengths. The point of a woman's talk is to talk, not to solve problems.

This is good news for men – it means that most of the time you're not expected to respond, just to listen. When a woman has finished speaking she feels relieved and happy. Plus she'll think you're a wonderful man for listening, so you'll probably have a good night!

GABS.

Chapter 2

Spatial Ability

"Oh no! I can't believe this ... look at this map! ... I think we were supposed to turn right at that big green mountain ..."

Knowing What's What and Where's Where

Reading maps and understanding where you are relies on spatial ability. Brain scans show that spatial ability is located in the right front brain for most men and boys, and is one of a male's strongest brain skills. It developed from ancient times to allow men, the hunters, to calculate the speed, movement and distance of prey, work out how fast they had to run to catch their targets, and know how much force they needed to kill it with a rock or a spear.

Spatial ability is located in both brain hemispheres for women but does not have a specific measurable location as it does in males. Only about 20% of women have good or excellent spatial ability and around 80% of women have limited spatial ability when compared to men.

Spatial ability means being able to picture, in the mind, the shape of things, their dimensions, co-ordinates, proportions, movement and geography. It also involves being able to imagine an object being rotated in space, navigating around an obstacle

course and seeing things from a three-dimensional perspective. With males, these are brain functions located in at least four sites in the right brain hemisphere.

Not having comparable spatial ability means that most women generally score on the low side with spatial activities and don't pursue careers or pastimes that require them such as air-traffic controllers, engineers, racing car drivers and pilots.

The following quizzes will tell you whether your spatial ability and your navigation skills are high or low and whether you fit the common clichés about men and women.

Test Your Spatial Skills

The following spatial test requires the same skills as reading a map or street directory, landing a plane or chasing a buffalo. Your brain has to imagine the image in three dimensions and then rotate it to get the correct angle.

Test 1

Imagine that the puzzle below was made of cardboard. If you were to fold it along the join lines it would make a cube with symbols around the outside. Assuming that the face with the circle is on the right and the square is on the left, which of your options A, B, C or D is the correct one?

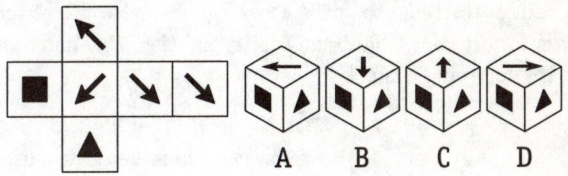

Test 2

Now here's a more complex version of the test that requires your brain to make even more spatial rotations.

Again, imagine that the puzzle was made of cardboard and you were to fold a cube. Which of your options A, B, C or D would it look like?

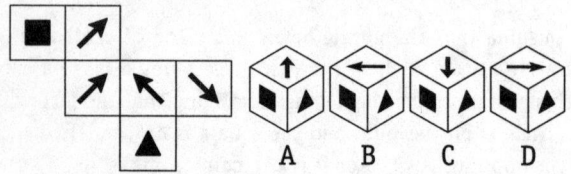

Besides tests like the ones above, you can also use matchsticks to test your logical and spatial abilities. Why don't you try the following examples:

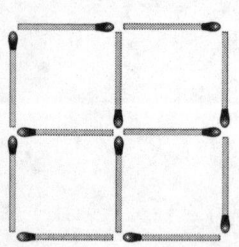

Test 3
How can you make three squares out of these four without removing a match?

Test 4
Now, remove three matches from the last test and then form three squares with the remaining ones.

Test 5
How can you form three equilateral triangles with six matches?

Test 6

In the following figure, thirteen matches form six areas of equal size. Remove one match and regroup the remaining matches so that they again form six areas of equal size.

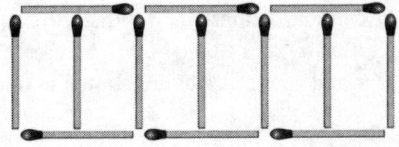

Test 7

In the following figure, six matches form five squares. Move two matches so that only three squares remain.

Test 8

Use twelve matches to form a figure that has twelve right angle corners.

If you cannot solve one question or the other right away or are not sure whether you have really formed the right figure, don't look up the solutions immediately. Don't give up too easily but try to crack the solution yourself. Sleep on it and try again the next day – it's worth it!

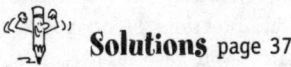

Solutions page 37

Test Your Ability to Read Maps and Your Navigational Skills

As theory is of little use without practice, we now test how well you can use your navigational skills and your ability to read maps in daily situations. In the first part you have to analyse and estimate your abilities, in the second part you need knowledge and your sense of orientation to find the right answers.

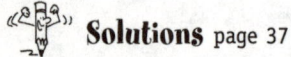

Solutions page 37

Part 1

In the questions below, tick the answer that comes closest to your behaviour in the described situations.

1. **You are going south in your car and have to find a certain road on the map. How do you proceed?**
   a) You take a short glance at the map and know immediately which way to go.
   b) You stare silently at the map for several minutes, turn it upside down, so that it is facing in the same direction as you are driving. But even now you find it difficult to find the road.
   c) You have to study the map carefully and turn it a bit in all directions before you find the street. Sometimes you have no success at all and ask somebody else for help.

2. **You are sight seeing with a tourist party. You have been walking around the city for the whole morning when one of your fellow travellers asks in which direction the castle is.**
   a) Without hesitation you point to the north and show them the way.
   b) You remember that the castle is in the top-left corner of your map but cannot point in the right direction.
   c) You know that the castle is in the north of the city and after orientating yourself by the sun and your current location, you point in roughly the right direction.

3. **You are in a huge stadium to watch a football match. At one point you go to buy some food. How long does it take you to get back to your seat?**
   a) Not long because you know exactly where your seat is.
   b) It might take a long time as you are likely to take the wrong way back and wander around aimlessly.
   c) If you remember the block you were sitting in, then you find your way without problems.

4. You have bought a DVD/Video player and want to program it according to the operating instructions. Do you succeed at the first attempt?
   a) Absolutely!
   b) No, at some point you have to take a break or give up.
   c) It takes you a while and you have to read some of the instructions several times, but you usually succeed.

5. You have left your street directory at home, but spot a public map in the city centre that shows the street you are looking for. What happens next?
   a) You take a brief look at the map and can find the way afterwards without problems.
   b) You try to remember the way according to the map but have forgotten it after two hundred metres.
   c) You have to look at the map for some time to remember the way. You try to memorise it, using prominent buildings (church, Town Hall etc.) and this works.

6. Were you good at maths in school?
   a) Yes, and you always liked the lessons.
   b) No, you were lousy, especially in geometry.
   c) Not too bad. You were quite good at some things but found others quite difficult.

7. **You have lost your way and ask a passer-by for directions. He explains it quickly. Do you find your destination?**
   a) Yes, because you have mentally 'saved' his words.
   b) No, because after a short time you cannot remember for sure whether you have to turn right or left.
   c) Usually yes, but if the explanation was too complicated you have difficulty.

8. **If you were in a room without windows, could you tell where North was?**
   a) Yes, without any problems.
   b) No, never.
   c) Probably, if you think about it for a while.

9. **You are moving. The furniture removalist wants to know where to put the sideboard in the dining room. How do you proceed?**
   a) You look at the sideboard and know immediately whether or not it will fit next to the kitchen door.
   b) You measure the sideboard carefully and write down the figures, because you will have forgotten them by the time you are in the house. You then measure the space next to the kitchen door.
   c) You take a long look at the sideboard and try to remember how wide the space in the dining room is. If you are not certain you start measuring or use your arms to measure the space and your hips to measure height.

10. You drive to a large shopping centre and park in a multi-level car park. Do you later find your car without problems?
   a) Not a problem, you don't even have to think about where it is parked.
   b) No, you probably have to wander through several levels until you find it.
   c) Because you feel confident, you remember the level number but you may possibly walk in the wrong direction when you return.

Part 2

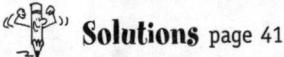

Solutions page 41

1. Which of the following illustrations shows the correct outline of Italy?

2. You are travelling through England and are driving on a country road from Hull in the East to Liverpool in the West. If you want to make a detour to London (in the South), do you have to turn right or left?
    a) Right
    b) Left

3. You are driving along a four-lane street in a city in a northerly direction. You want to turn left, which is not possible. You take a right turn at the next junction, and turn right again. Unfortunately you then have to turn left again because you have come to a one-way street. In which direction are you now driving?
    a) North
    b) East
    c) South
    d) West

4. This map shows the United Kingdom. Which way is north? Please mark in the compass.

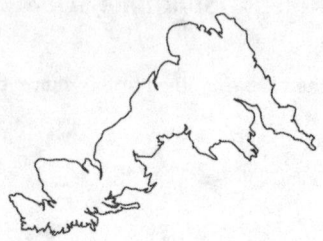

5. Which country does this illustration show? And what is special about it?

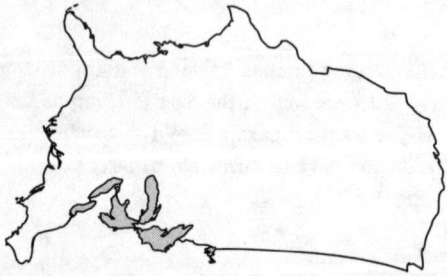

6. You are driving in a southerly direction. First you turn right, then left. After a sharp bend to the right (90 degrees) you turn left twice and have reached your destination. In which direction are you now looking when you look in the rear-view mirror.
   a) To the North
   b) To the East
   c) To the South
   d) To the West

7. Here you see an illustration of Australia. Mark the capital, Canberra.

8. You are visiting friends in Madrid. You are standing on the balcony, looking in the direction of Granada to the east. Barcelona is to the North so is it to your right or to your left?
   a) Right
   b) Left

9. Which of these illustrations shows Africa correctly oriented?

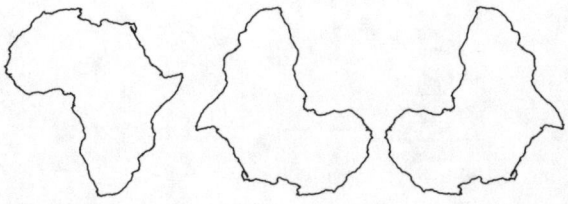

10. You are driving in Malta on the left side. Coming from the north you turn right. At the third junction you turn left and reverse park so that your car is rear-to-kerb. In which direction does your car's hood face?
    a) North
    b) East
    c) South
    d) West

Solutions

Test Your Spatial Skills

Compare your solutions with the answers below. If you have solved all tasks correctly your spatial skills are excellent. Only a few incorrect answers or unsolved tasks still indicates good to very good spatial skills. Those who could only solve some or none of the tasks, have poor spatial skills.

Test 1
B

Test 2
A

Test 3

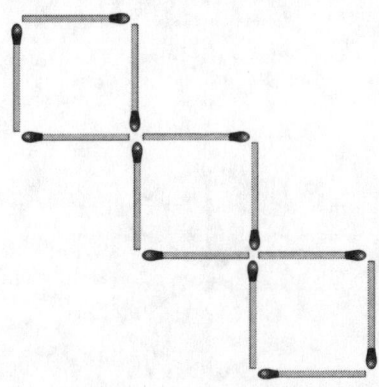

Test 4

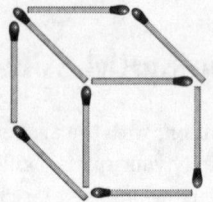

Test 5

The three matches in the basic triangle have to meet in the middle and make up a three-dimensional figure.

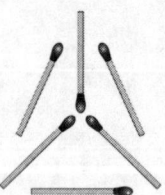

Test 6

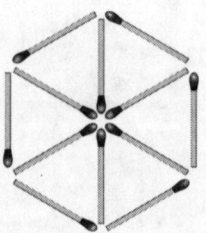

Test 7

By moving the two matches you get three squares (and two rectangles).

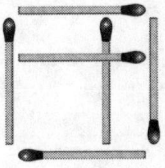

Test 8

The Figure should look like this:

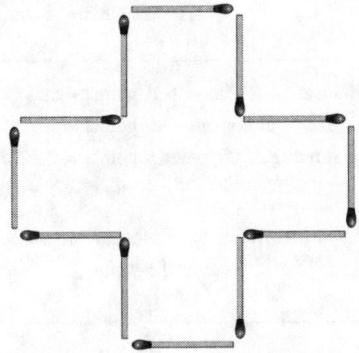

Test Your Ability to Read Maps and Your Navigational Skills

Part 1

First, add the number of A, B and C responses and use the following table to arrive at your final result.

For Females:

Number of A's times (-5) points = ...
Number of B's times 15 points = ...
Number of C's times 5 points = ...
Total points = ...

For Males:

Number of A's times (-5) points = ...
Number of B's times 10 points = ...
Number of C's times 5 points = ...
Total points = ...

*If you are unable to answer any question,
award yourself 5 points.*

Most males will score between 0 – 180 and most females, 150 – 300. People who do not show significantly good or poor spatial abilities achieve scores between 150–180. Keep in mind that there are always exceptions to the rule.

A man with good spatial abilities usually scores lower than 150 points. The closer to 0 the better his navigational skills and spatial abilities. A woman with poor spatial abilities usually scores higher than 180. The higher her score, the poorer her navigational skills and her ability to read maps. Scores between 150 – 180 show compatibility of thought for both sexes and demonstrate a high flexibility of thinking.

Part 2

Compare your solutions with those below. Use the same criteria for evaluation as with the tests for spatial skills.

1. b

2. b
3. b
4.

5. It's a mirror image of The United States.

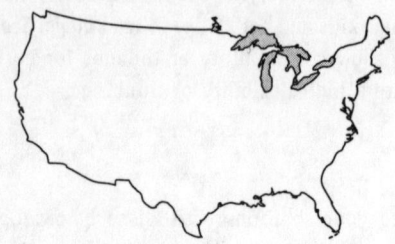

6. d – to the West
7.

8. b – the Left
9. a

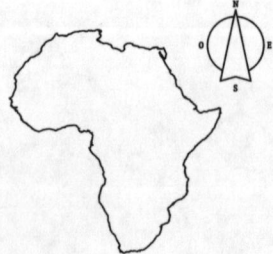

10. d – to the West

Test Evaluation

If you are a woman who achieved poor results here, don't be concerned. If you are a man with good results, don't feel smug.

From an evolutionary perspective, being able to chase animals and find the way home was never part of a woman's job description. This is why many women today still have trouble reading a map or street directory and finding their way around.

Male superiority in spatial skills is no great surprise, considering male evolution as hunters. Men are good at estimating speed, distance, angles and directions and they use these same inborn skills in reading maps and finding their way.

Spatial ability allows a man to rotate a map in his mind and know in which direction to go. If he has to return to the same location at a later time, he doesn't need the map as his spatial areas can store the information. Most males can read a map while facing north, even though the map tells them to travel south. Studies also show that a man's brain measures speed and distance to know when to change direction.

Women have more connections between their left and right brain hemispheres through a thicker corpus callosum so women tend to be more ambidextrous than men; and three times as many women have difficulty in instantly knowing their left hand from their right hand.

Most women have difficulty when reading and navigating with maps because they need a three-dimensional perspective. Men have the ability to turn a two-dimensional map into a three-dimensional view in their mind, but most women have difficulty with this task. However, if they use a three-dimensional perspective map, women dramatically improve their navigational skills. But unlike men, they are usually not able to convert sounds and signals into three-dimensional mind maps to visualise the correct direction and route to take.

Can You Improve Your Spatial Skills?

In a word – yes. You can constantly practise your spatial activities until your brain develops sufficient connections to do the task. Be prepared for the long haul with this one, though. It is now clear that practice and repetition help permanently to create more brain connections for a given task.

Learning and practising how to read maps can greatly increase your practical ability to use them, just as daily practice on the piano makes for more competent playing. However, regular practice is required to maintain a reasonable level. Unless the piano player or map reader keeps practicing, their skill level will diminish quickly and take longer to recover than a person whose brain is wired to handle the task.

Alternative Strategies

If these methods seem too difficult, there are alternative strategies that might be worth thinking about. When men stop asking women to navigate, everyone's lives become happier; when women stop criticising men's driving ability, there are far fewer arguments. We are all good at different things so if you are not good at a particular task, don't worry about it. You can improve with practice but don't let it ruin your life or that of your partner.

To have a happy life as a man: Never insist that a woman reads a map or a street directory. And as a woman, you should let him find the way in future – it's as easy as that!

Chapter 3

Parking and Driving

A Sunday drive with your wife...

Each According to Their Own

When driving a car the spatial abilities between the sexes become apparent, whether it's about women being worse at parking a car or reading maps or about men who will not ask for directions when they are lost.

Any husband who teaches his wife to drive is heading for the divorce courts. Driving a car is a test of a man's spatial ability relative to the environment. A woman's objective in driving is to get safely from point A to point B and she realises she doesn't have to beat her best personal time. A man's best strategy as a passenger is to close his eyes, turn up the radio and stop making comments because, overall, women are safer drivers than men. She'll get him to their destination – it may just take a little longer. But at least he can relax and arrive alive.

A woman will criticise a man's driving because his spatial ability allows him to make decisions and judgements that seem dangerous to her. Provided he doesn't have a poor driving record, she also needs to relax and not criticise, and just let him do the driving.

As you can see, men and women have contrasting qualifications for driving cars and from time to time this leads to the obvious differences in how they drive, in their reactions to certain incidents and the extremely tricky issue of reverse parking a car.

At First Sight

If you were asked to look at cars that had been parallel parked in a street, could you tell which cars had been parked by men and which by women? Could you tell from the way they drive on a winding road whether it's a man or a woman behind the wheel of the car in front of you? We are certain you can, and in most cases, even at first sight.

Now put yourself to the test and answer the following questions about driving and parking. Here you will not only find out what kind of drivers you and your partner are, but also learn interesting details about yourself and your behaviour. Remember – for each phenomenon there is also an explanation. Read the evaluation of the test carefully and remember it when the way your partner drives the car sends you mad.

The Great Test of Driving and Parking

You probably remember taking your first driving test. You probably had sweaty hands, hoping that your driving instructor's lively discussion would distract the examiner's attention away from your daring overtaking manoeuvres or that you would be spared reverse parking. But don't worry – we won't put you to the test again to certify whether you rightfully got your driving licence or whether it seems more likely that you won it in the lottery.

You will now find out whether you behave in a typically male or female way when driving and the evaluation will also tell you why this is so.

1. **You are driving along a country road on a dull winter's day, when it starts to drizzle. What do you do?**
    a) You turn on the wipers as soon as the first drop of rain hits the windscreen and set the wiper to the highest level. After all, you need clear sight, especially when it rains. (Type C)
    b) You switch on the windscreen wiper and experiment with the setting until it fits the amount of water on the screen. (Type A)
    c) You wait until the exact amount of raindrops relative to the speed of the wipers are on the windscreen and turn the wipers on. (Type B)

2. **After an exhausting day at work you get home and are out of luck: all parking spaces in your road and the adjacent ones are occupied. What do you do?**
   a) You drive round the block for a while. After all, there's a good song on the radio. When you still haven't found a space you park on the pavement – hoping that the traffic warden won't come along that night. (Type C)
   b) You are hungry and tired and want to get home as quickly as possible but you don't fancy looking for a parking space. You stop your car next to the parked ones and read the newspaper until somebody drives off. (Type B)
   c) In your opinion, parallel parking should be prohibited anyway. If necessary, you will therefore park half a kilometre from home on a public parking lot, because you know that there's always enough space there. (Type A)

3. **You are driving on your own to visit friends who have recently moved. What do you do when you realise that you have lost your way?**
   a) As you are on your own, you can't possibly read the map and drive at the same time. Anyway, you would not be able to find your position on the map quickly enough. You start looking for passers-by and ask them for directions – the residents surely know their way around the area better than you do. (Type A)
   b) As soon as possible you drive to the side of the road and stop the car to take a look at the map and find out where you have taken the wrong turn. After all, you want to get to your friend's place as soon as possible and don't want to lose precious time by aimless searching. (Type C)
   c) Instead of asking somebody else for directions, you follow your instincts and keep going in the direction you think is right. Sooner or later you will find your way. After all, this has always worked and your tank is still nearly full. (Type B)

4. **You drive to the supermarket but the parking lot is full. Along the road you find a free space and reverse into it. What happens?**
   a) Your car sits far away from the kerb, but as you want to buy just one loaf of bread you don't really mind. After all, you will be back in no time. (Type C)
   b) Your car is parked the perfect distance from the kerb – just like it always is. (Type B)
   c) You need three attempts to get into the parking space and you have to drive forwards and backwards a few times until the car is parked correctly. You decide that next time you will wait for a free space on the parking lot.(Type A)

5. **How do you usually behave as a front-seat passenger?**
   a) You let the other person drive and don't comment on his or her driving. When he or she asks you to find the right way, you read the map well and look out for the next junction. Apart from that, you don't interfere. (Type C)
   b) You give instructions like "Turn left – slow down – change gears – watch out for the car ahead – can you see the pedestrian over there?" because it makes you nervous when you don't drive yourself. After all, you can never know whether the driver would react as fast and as well as you would. (Type B)
   c) You feel a little uneasy because you would drive more carefully and you worry that the driver will not be able to react fast enough to possible danger. You therefore remind him/her a few times

not to drive so fast and to keep a greater distance between cars. (Type A)

6. **You are taking your dog for a walk when somebody asks you for directions to the nearest doctor's surgery. How do you describe the way?**
   a) Although you have noticed the sign to the practice a few times and can remember the doctor's name, you cannot tell which street it's in. Because you don't want to seem impolite, you wave your hand in the approximate direction you have just come from and say with an apologetic smile: "I think it's this way, but maybe you should take the bus, it's quite a way to walk". (Type C)
   b) You explain the way as you remember it. "Up there you turn right . . . or was it left? Anyway, at the corner you can see a shoe shop and that's the street you have to turn into. And after about five houses there's an Italian restaurant that used to be a Kebab House, but that's not it yet, the surgery is after the next junction on the opposite side of the street." (Type A)
   c) You think about it briefly, then you explain the shortest way to the practice by giving exact details: "You walk about three hundred metres along High Street in a southerly direction, then turn right into Hill Street. You cross the street at the third set of traffic lights and walk another fifty metres. That's where the surgery is". (Type B)

7. **You are going along the motorway with your partner (who is driving) and are talking about your nosy neighbour while Madonna's latest song is on the radio. A short distance before the next motorway intersection, your partner asks you to look at the map and tell him/her which exit you have to take. What do you do?**
   a) You keep on talking but switch off the radio before you take a short look at the map and explain the way. (Type B)
   b) You immediately stop talking, take a long look at the map and turn it upside down or around in order to find the right way. (Type A)
   c) You hum along with Madonna – loudly and off key – glance at the map but then orientate yourself by the road signs. (Type C)

8. **Imagine you are a member of the City Council and are deciding what the parking lot of the new shopping centre should look like. How would you vote?**
   a) You vote for a spaciously planned car park, with spaces that are wide enough for a seven-ton truck, where you can not only park forwards without any difficulty but also drive off just as easily. You don't mind that a few additional driving lanes are necessary. After all, it's not your money that is being spent. (Type A)
   b) You vote for a sufficient number of parking spaces, to make the situation for the shop's customers as relaxed as possible. From your own experience you know how unpleasant the usual fights for parking spaces on a Saturday morning

are. After all, you have lost more than one. (Type C)

c) You don't really care about the car park. You don't have any problems with parking, and those who do should go shopping somewhere else. You are more interested in possible tax benefits for the city. (Type B)

9. **Coming back from a trip one Sunday afternoon, you spot a free parking space right in front of your house. However, it is quite tight. What do you do?**
   a) You park there no matter how tight the spot is. After all, you have to take a gift, especially when it's handed to you on a plate. You'd rather drive forwards and backwards a few times than walk further than is absolutely necessary. (Type B)
   b) You're really not in the mood to squeeze into the tight space right now, so you'd rather take the larger one you have just spotted at the other end of the road. You park there even though you know you will barely be able to feel your feet in your new leather boots as you walk the extra distance. (Type C)
   c) You know that your front-seat passenger will come close to a nervous breakdown if you haven't safely manoeuvred the car into the parking space after the third attempt, so you decide it's better to let him park the car – that way you can at least get to the bathroom sooner than you expected. (Type A)

10. **You have to go to a meeting in a city you have never been to. The meeting will take place in a huge conference centre and you have to drive there on your own. How do you prepare for the drive?**
   a) You don't. You know that the meeting will take place in the south of the city and you are sure that there will be more than enough signs pointing you to the conference centre. After all, it's a well-known location just outside the city. (Type B)
   b) You read the map carefully before you start your trip and try to memorise the way. During the drive, you have the map ready at hand on the passenger's seat so you can take a quick look in case of emergency. (Type C)
   c) You ask somebody to explain the way and write down all crossroads where you have to turn off. Or you print out a detailed description from the internet and stick right to it even if road signs point you in different directions. (Type A)

11. Late at night you approach a junction. A foreign car is already waiting at the red traffic light with a blinking indicator. The green arrow for cars turning right can barely be seen in the dark. Obviously the other car's driver has not seen it. What do you do?
    a) You slow down and come to a halt behind the car. If it doesn't move you sound the horn once and try to draw the driver's attention to the green arrow. (Type C)
    b) You keep on going, switch to the free lane for cars turning left, go round the waiting car, tapping your forehead to show the other driver what you think about his driving skills. (Type B)
    c) You stop behind the waiting car and wait until the traffic lights switch to green. First of all, you are not in a hurry, secondly, something similar has happened to you and thirdly you are neither a road safety trainer nor a school teacher. (Type A)

12. You want to drive to work but realise that the car in front of you is parked so close to yours that you will have problems getting your car out. How do you proceed to manoeuvre the car as quickly as possible out of the parking space?

a) You turn the steering wheel as far in the direction of the kerb as it will go and reverse as far as possible, checking alternately in the rear-view and the side mirrors to accurately judge the distance from the car behind you. Then you turn the wheel fully in the opposite direction and go forward. This way you edge your way slowly out of the space. (Type A)

b) You reverse straight as far as possible. Only then do you turn the steering wheel towards the street and go forwards as far as possible. Then you turn it fully in the direction of the kerb and reverse. You briefly open the door or even get out to check the distance to the car behind you. Eventually, you manoeuvre out of the space. (Type B)

c) You reverse until you touch the car behind you. Going forward you do the same. This way you use the space most efficiently. The owners of the other cars better not complain, after all, it was they who parked you in. (Type C)

13. You are in France, on your way to a holiday resort, driving in bright sunshine along a country road. Your front-seat passenger has fallen asleep over the map and after passing through a number of roundabouts, you have lost your orientation and are not sure whether you're still going in the right direction. What do you do?
    a) You orientate without problems by using the sun and instantly know that you are still going south. So at least the main direction is right. (Type B)
    b) You keep going until you pass the next road sign, trying to remember what the name of the next bigger city should be. If you are not successful this way, you try to orientate by the sun and succeed after some difficulty. (Type C)
    c) With the best will in the world you don't know where to go and – with some regrets – wake up your passenger so they can help you. (Type A)

14. You are going along the motorway and hear on the radio that there is a traffic jam fifteen minutes ahead of you. You could take the next exit and use the winding country road to get home. What do you do?
    a) You are happy that even before the exit there is a motorway service area. Your car could use filling and you're feeling a little hungry, so you decide to make the best out of the situation, have something to eat and get some rest while the others are waiting in the traffic jam. (Type C)
    b) You leave the motorway and take the country road. Rounding the bends at a fast speed, you will be home not much later than via the motorway. (Type A)
    c) You carefully weigh up the possibilities. You do not like to go along winding roads, and will probably decide to stay on the motorway hoping that the jam will break up soon, so you don't have to wait too long. (Type B)

15. **You are driving in dense traffic on a double-track street right through the city. Your colleague, whom you want to drop off at the station, is furiously telling you about his problems with his boss and asks for your advice. What do you do?**

   a) You tell your colleague that right now you have to concentrate fully on the traffic and thus cannot pay enough attention to him. You offer to call him in the evening and support him with advice. (Type B)

   b) You keep a greater distance to the car in front of you and slow down a bit because you can discuss your colleague's problem better when you are able to look at him now and then. Although he is your friend, you do not want to risk an accident because of him. (Type C)

   c) You keep going as before and are able to concentrate equally well on the traffic and your colleague's problems. You give him sound advice while talking or shouting now and then at other drivers who change lanes all the time to make faster progress. (Type A)

Evaluation

Now count how often you chose type A, B and C. Each answer is one point. Read the category below where you scored the highest points.

Type A

You clearly are a female type of driver. You often have problems with parking, especially when the space is tight. Somehow you never get the angle right and you are poor at judging when to turn the wheel left or right and how far. Your sense of orientation is not the best either.

This has always been a problem for you and you wonder why. Here's the answer – while testosterone will improve spatial ability, the female hormone, oestrogen, suppresses it. Women have dramatically less testosterone than men and, as a result, the more feminine the brain, the weaker the spatial ability. This is why very feminine women are not great parallel parkers or map readers.

The same is true when you have to describe a route or give detailed directions to a woman. Never give directions to a woman like, "Head north" or "Go west for five kilometres" as this requires compass skills. Instead, give directions involving landmarks such as "Drive past McDonald's and head for the building with the National Bank sign on top." This allows a woman to pick up these landmarks with her peripheral vision and head straight toward them.

Besides, women are more judicious, foresighted and careful drivers than men and always stick to the road rules. Women simply want nothing else but to get from one place to another, safely and in comfort.

Type B

You clearly are a male type of driver. Thanks to your good spatial skills you don't have any problems parking your car and even see tight spaces as just another challenge. You see driving as fun and you like to try things that take you or your car to the limits.

Men love to drive fast around winding roads because their spatial skills come into play – gear ratios, clutch and brake combinations, relative speed to corners, angles and distances.

Your exceptionally well-developed sense of direction and orientation has never let you down so far, but your verbal skills are inferior compared to those of women. This explains why you have difficulty concentrating on driving while talking at the same time, especially when heavy traffic demands your full attention. You switch off the radio when you are looking for directions and you do not mumble while thinking (as many women do) but tend to keep quiet.

Type C

You show neither clear male nor distinctly female characteristics in driving, but sit somewhere in the middle. You have a flexibility of thinking, which is often an advantage, because you always treat problems in a very pragmatic way. You always think about your actions, for example, when the parking space right in front of your door was tight but there was a larger one a few hundred metres down the road.

You don't shy away from asking for help when you have, for example, lost your way, but nevertheless (and that shows your male side) you try to find the way on your own at first.

Science research has shown that women can learn how to park a car; parking tests at driving schools show that women generally do better at reverse parking than men during driver training, but statistics show women perform poorly in real life situations and you can probably confirm this from your own experience. This is because women are better than men at learning a task and successfully repeating it, provided the environment and conditions under which they do it don't change. In traffic, however, every situation presents a new set of data to be assessed and men's spatial ability is better suited to handle this task.

Chapter 4

The Opposite Sex

Waiting for Mr Right

How to Find the Right Partner

Love usually starts with lust, which can last a few hours, a few days or a few weeks. Next comes infatuation, which lasts, on average, three to twelve months before attachment takes over. When the blinding cocktail of hormones subsides after six to twelve months, we now see our partner in the cold light of day and those little habits we found so endearing at first begin to become irritating. Once you thought it was cute that he could never find things in the fridge or that he'd constantly lose his car keys, but now it makes you want to scream. He used to love hearing you talk all night about every little thing but now he's contemplating murder. You silently ask yourself, "Can I live like this for the rest of my life? What do we have in common?"

Chances are you don't have much in common or much to talk about. Mother Nature's objective is to throw men and women together under the influence of a powerful hormonal cocktail that causes them to procreate and not think. Finding the right partner means deciding what things you want to have in common with someone in the long term, and to do this in advance of nature's blinding hormonal highs. When the

infatuation stage has passed – and pass it will – can you maintain a lasting relationship based on friendship and common interests? Write a list of the traits and interests you want in a long-term partner and then you'll know exactly who you are looking for. A man will have a list of qualities for his ideal mate but when he goes to a party, his brain is fired up by testosterone. It then searches for the 'ideal' woman based on hormonal motivation – nice legs, flat stomach, round buttocks, good boobs, and so on; all features connected with short-term procreation. Women want a man who is sensitive and caring, has a V-shaped torso and a fun personality, all things connected to child-rearing, animal-chasing and protecting. These are also short-term biological needs and have little to do with success in a 21st Century relationship. When you write a list of the desirable long-term characteristics in your perfect partner and keep it handy, it helps you to be objective about a new person the next time nature tries to control your thoughts and urges with hormones.

Nature wants you to procreate as often as possible and it uses powerful drugs to push you into it. When you understand this and are armed with a job description of your ideal long-term mate, you are less likely to be biologically tricked and are more likely to be successful in your hunt for that elusive perfect partner with whom you'll finally be able to live happily ever after.

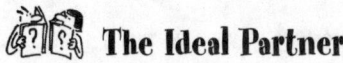 The Ideal Partner

No matter whether you are currently in a relationship or are still looking for the perfect partner, you should start now by getting your wishes, dreams and preferences clear in your mind. You can take the following quiz either on your own or together with your partner and compare results – it will be informative either way.

There is no evaluation for this quiz – after all, it is designed as a means for you to learn how to evaluate yourself and your desires. Only you can determine what the descriptions of similar, balanced or contrasting interests might mean for you and your relationship.

Tick all features that apply to you and that you consider important in your partner.

Outward appearance or other things you consider important in your partner:

- ❑ ❑ figure/physique
- ❑ ❑ well-groomed appearance
- ❑ ❑ beautiful hands
- ❑ ❑ height
- ❑ ❑ smoker
- ❑ ❑ no paunch or beard
- ❑ ❑ level of education
- ❑ ❑ profession
- ❑ ❑ good sex
- ❑ ❑ bosom
- ❑ ❑ bottom
- ❑ ❑ muscles
- ❑ ❑ long/short hair
- ❑ ❑ non-smoker
- ❑ ❑ circle of friends/family
- ❑ ❑ attractive appearance
- ❑ ❑ beautiful eyes
- ❑ ❑ solvency

other:

....

Character traits that are important in your partner:

- ❏ ❏ humour
- ❏ ❏ willingness to compromise
- ❏ ❏ spontaneity
- ❏ ❏ sporting activity
- ❏ ❏ social activity
- ❏ ❏ personality
- ❏ ❏ intelligence
- ❏ ❏ empathy
- ❏ ❏ adaptability
- ❏ ❏ loyalty
- ❏ ❏ tolerance
- ❏ ❏ patience
- ❏ ❏ love of animals
- ❏ ❏ flexibility
- ❏ ❏ parenthood
- ❏ ❏ independence
- ❏ ❏ honesty
- ❏ ❏ devotion
- ❏ ❏ politics
- ❏ ❏ generosity
- ❏ ❏ religion
- ❏ ❏ fidelity
- ❏ ❏ restraint
- ❏ ❏ emotions

....

....

....

Your own interests and what is important to you:

- ❏ ❏ travelling
- ❏ ❏ good food
- ❏ ❏ good wine
- ❏ ❏ holiday by the sea
- ❏ ❏ holiday in the mountains
- ❏ ❏ literature
- ❏ ❏ city life
- ❏ ❏ pleasantness
- ❏ ❏ religion
- ❏ ❏ cinema/film
- ❏ ❏ music
- ❏ ❏ culture
- ❏ ❏ career/success at work
- ❏ ❏ country life/nature

....
....
....

Your hobbies or past-times:

....
....
....
....
....
....

Is Your Relationship Intact?

Are you now, after years, still as much in love as on the first day? Or has a daily grind crept silently into your relationship? How do things look for your great love? Are you feeling completely confident or are you wondering whether it all makes sense?

Put your relationship to the test. Our merciless reality check shows you if there is a problem. Tick each of the following statements that you agree with.

1. ❏ Your relationship has lost its charm.
2. ❏ You haven't gone on a spontaneous trip for a long time.
3. ❏ Your feelings for your partner have weakened.
4. ❏ You rarely sleep with each other.
5. ❏ Recently your partner's weaknesses seem to bother you more than they used to.
6. ❏ You go out with friends more often – each of you with their own friends.
7. ❏ Your partner increasingly criticizes you in front of others.
8. ❏ You haven't been really happy in a long time.
9. ❏ You are frequently feeling misunderstood.
10. ❏ Your partner hasn't thought of something special for your birthday in a long time.
11. ❏ You argue more and more often for the slightest reason.

12. ❑ Recently, your partner comes home late and then goes straight to bed.
13. ❑ In arguments you seem to become more and more unforgiving.
14. ❑ Sometimes you feel treated unfairly.
15. ❑ You don't talk as much with each other as you used to.
16. ❑ On Saturdays you nearly always rent a video and stay at home.
17. ❑ You hardly ever caress each other.
18. ❑ You envy your friend's partners.
19. ❑ Your partner hasn't paid you compliments or said something nice in a long time.
20. ❑ You both increasingly go your own ways.

The Great Romance Test

Are you a hopelessly romantic person who would like to embrace the whole world all at once when in love and who sees the world through rose-coloured glasses? Or are you rather a rational realist who has never heard of the word 'romance' and who seldom comes out of their shell? This test will help you find out which type you are.

Tick the statements that fit you best. For each question tick one answer only.

1. What is your opinion on the topic 'sex and love'?
 a) Sex is sex and love is love and in some exceptional cases both occur at the same time. (Type C)
 b) True love? In your opinion it's only sentimental mush. There just is no such thing as true love. (Type D)
 c) For you sex and love are inextricably linked with each other. (Type A)
 d) Sex is most fulfilling when true feelings are at play – but without them it is not to be detested either. (Type B)

2. What would you consider a romantic weekend for two?
 a) It could be a romantic trip to a city, a trip to a lake or a hiking-tour in the mountains. (Type B)
 b) It means that you do a lot of things you would not normally do just for your partner's sake so you can have good sex afterwards. (Type C)

    c) A short holiday in a snow-covered hotel in the Alps, with a sleigh ride in moonlight under a clear starry sky, a romantic candlelight dinner, and afterwards snuggling up together in front of the fire. (Type A)

    d) Nothing much, because it has to do with seclusion and togetherness. And that's just not your cup of tea. (Type D)

3. Do you find it easy to say, "I love you"?

    a) You find it quite difficult, but to please your partner you say it sometimes – often after he or she asks you to. (Type C)

    b) Absolutely! If you love your partner you cannot tell them often enough. (Type A)

    c) You think something like this should not be said carelessly. Therefore you say it sparingly, but when you do it comes from the bottom of your heart. (Type B)

    d) No. You hate declarations of love. (Type D)

4. Your partner asks you to put on some romantic music. Which would you choose?

    a) There is no sentimental crooning in your house. (Type D)

    b) Depending on your mood it might be classic or pop music, something that means a lot to both of you. (Type B)

    c) A CD you bought just for your partner and would not listen to on your own. (Type C)

    d) The more sentimental and soppy, the better. You want to enjoy your cuddly mood to the full. (Type A)

5. What does marriage mean to you?
a) Marriage is the price you have to pay for regular sex. (Type D)
b) It's the fulfilment and goal of every happy relationship. (Type A)
c) A meaningful institution that allows you to express your love. (Type B)
d) Sex is the price you have to pay for marriage. (Type C)

6. How would you judge a little infidelity?
a) It's an unforgivable breach of faith and therefore a reason for separation. (Type A)
b) If two people really love each other and are happy in their relationship, neither of them should have a cause for an infidelity. It is therefore an indicator that something's wrong in the relationship. Depending on the gravity, you could be willing to forgive it. (Type B)
c) You don't consider it a big problem. It does not have anything to do with your partner either. Sometimes you just need a bit of variety – and the wind of change has never done a relationship any harm. (Type D)
d) You stick to the saying "What the eye does not see the heart cannot grieve over" and would neither admit to nor want to be told about an infidelity. (Type C)

7. What do you do if your partner asks you to show him or her more affection?
a) You empty the rubbish bin, buy a bunch of flowers, put a new roll of toilet paper into the

holder, wash the car, collect laundry from the drycleaner's or cook something nice. Which of these things you do doesn't matter. For you they all mean the same. It's most important that at least you do something. (Type C)

b) Your partner would never say that, because you regularly set something up to surprise them, for example a little treat that shows how much they mean to you. (Type A)

c) You tell him/her that lots of affection is Hollywood hype. If you didn't love him/her, you wouldn't be together. (Type D)

d) You excuse yourself for having been so thoughtless recently and ask for his/her concrete wishes and fulfil them as soon as possible. (Type B)

8. **At the beginning of your relationship the days (and nights) were just not long enough. You spent so many hours holding hands, stroking each other's back and talking endlessly. But now you are married and things have changed. What do you think is the reason?**

a) You can't really explain it yourself. Your partner seems to be the one who grows reticent and does not say why. Recently you get the feeling that he/she does not love you (any more). (Type A)

b) By now you know everything you have to know about your partner. It just doesn't make much sense any more to talk to each other for hours. (Type D)

c) That's the way things are; as long as you get along well and everything is alright in bed, you are not really worried. (Type C)

    d) You think it's a pity. Now and then you try to change matters. But probably it's like the first phase of being in love: at some point this exceptional state is over. (Type B)

9. For you, infatuation is . . .
    a) Nothing more than nature's biological trick to guarantee that a man and a woman are thrown together long enough to procreate. (Type D)
    b) A matter judged too importantly, because it is never permanent and at some point the reality will hit really hard. (Type C)
    c) One of the greatest feelings of all. In the ideal case it could even last a whole lifetime, even if science claims the opposite. (Type A)
    d) Simply wonderful and should be enjoyed as long as possible. (Type B)

10. When you are in love . . .
    a) You walk around with a stupid smile on your face as if you are on remote control, floating above the ground, and are not able to make one clear thought. (Type A)
    b) Even serious every-day problems seem small and unimportant to you. You are full of energy and nothing can put you in a bad mood. (Type B)
    c) You feel extremely physically attracted to your partner and think about him/her – and making love with him/her – the whole day. (Type C)
    d) Being in love is nothing but extreme physical attraction – which of course is not negative at all. (Type D)

Evaluations

Is your Relationship Intact?

Count how many boxes you have ticked and read the corresponding section below.

0–5 Boxes Ticked

Everything in your relationship seems to be fine. Nevertheless, you should be careful and not lose sight of the beautiful moments of everyday life and togetherness because they make being together so valuable. Only those who can treasure the little moments of happiness can make their relationship last.

6–14 Boxes Ticked

Depending on whether you are in the upper or lower half of the scale, you should make your decisions with care. A clarifying talk about your future together and your ideas about your relationship might be a first step in the right direction. It is probably not too late and with some new ideas you can make your relationship exciting once again.

15–20 Boxes Ticked

Your relationship is really not blessed with good fortune any more. Obviously you and your partner have drifted apart. You have to consider very carefully whether you want to keep up this relationship – you're not doing yourself or him/her any favours.

The Great Romance Test

Count how often you chose type A, B, C and D. Each answer scores one point. Add the points for each type, then read the section below for the category that totalled the highest number of points.

Type A

You are hopelessly romantic. Even the thought of walking with your partner along a lonely beach, of a candlelight dinner or a traditional proposal – the man holding a red rose and kneeling down – makes your eyes moist and your knees shaky.

However, your romantic ideas dim your sense of reality occasionally or raise high expectations, which can lead to problems in your relationship – particularly if your partner is not the romantic type.

Type B

You are quite romantic but nonetheless have both feet firmly on the ground and seldom lose your grip on reality. This is a healthy balance and in most cases your partner will not disappoint you. For you, the concept of romance is not tied to certain clichés (walking in the moonlight, declarations of love, etc.) but evolves from a certain moment – and that's exactly what makes it so special to you.

Type C

You consider romance more of a means to an end, especially when you have a partner who is very romantic. You, however, are more of a realist – to get goose-pimples with emotion, pangs of happiness at the sight of an open fire or high levels of endorphins in the presence of a bridal couple is not in your nature – but if it makes your partner happy (and spares you discussions), you are willing to do what is necessary.

Type D

You really are not a romantic person at all and you don't try to hide it either – after all, you know that a leopard cannot change its spots, not even for the love of its partner. If anyone asks you, the whole concept of mushy romance should be put aside without any fuss. You consider most of it simply a ploy of Marketing experts (Valentine's Day is the obvious example – it must have been invented by a florist or a card manufacturer), but you are not going to fall for that!

With these extreme opinions, you should not be surprised that now and then you have to face nerve-wracking discussions, especially if your partner is very romantic.

How to Make Romance Run Smoothly

For those of you who rated poorly at our romance test – and that's usually more likely to be men than women – we have compiled six sure-fire romance tips that will show you how to wrap every woman around your little finger.

1. **Set the environment** – When you consider a woman's physical sensitivity to her surroundings and the high receptivity of her senses to outside stimuli, it makes sense that a man pays attention to the environment. Women's oestrogen hormones make her sensitive to the right lighting – dimly lit rooms make pupils dilate so that people look more attractive to each other and skin blemishes and wrinkles are less noticeable. A woman's superior hearing means the right music is important, and a clean, secure cave is better than one that can be invaded by children or other people at any moment. Women's insistence on sex in private explains why most women's private fantasy is of having sex in public, while a man's private fantasy is sex with a stranger.

2. **Feed her** – Having evolved as a lunch-chaser, you'd think it would occur to a man that providing a woman with food stirs up primal female feelings. This is why taking a woman to dinner is a significant event for her even when she's not hungry, because the provision of food shows his attention to her well-being and survival. Cooking a meal for a woman has an even deeper intrinsic meaning as it brings out primitive feelings in both a man and a woman.

3. **Light a fire** – Collecting wood and lighting a fire to give warmth and protection has been done by men for women for hundreds of thousands of years, and appeals to most women's romantic side. Even if it's a gas fire that she can light easily herself, he needs to light it if he wants to set a romantic atmosphere. The pay-off comes from the act of providing for her needs, not from the fire itself.

4. **Bring flowers** – Most men do not understand the power of a bunch of fresh flowers. Men think, "Why spend so much money on something that will be dead and thrown out in a few days?" It makes sense to a man's logical mind to give a woman a potted plant because, with constant care and attention, it will survive – in fact, you could even make a profit on it! However, a woman doesn't see it that way – she wants a bunch of fresh flowers. After a few days the flowers die and are thrown out, but this presents an opportunity for him to buy another bunch and once again bring out her romantic side by providing for her needs.

5. **Go dancing** – It's not that men don't want to dance, it's just that many of them don't have the necessary locations in either brain hemisphere to feel rhythm. Go to any aerobics class and watch the male participants (if any turn up) trying to keep time. When a man takes dancing lessons for basic rock 'n' roll and waltz, he will be the hit of the party with **all** women. Dancing has been described as a vertical act of horizontal desire and that's its actual history – it's a ritual that evolved to allow close male/female body contact as a lead-up to courtship, just as it does with other animals.

6. **Buy chocolates and champagne** – This combination has long been associated with romance, although few people know why. Champagne contains a chemical not found in other alcoholic beverages that increases women's testosterone level. Chocolate contains phenylethylamine, which stimulates the woman's love centre in the brain. Research by Danielle Piomella at the Neurosciences Institute in San Diego discovered three new chemicals called N-acylethanolamines, which attach themselves to the cannabis receptors in a woman's brain, giving her sensations similar to being high on marijuana. These chemicals are found in brown chocolate and cocoa, but not in white chocolate or coffee.

And to all women who – in contrast to their partners – turned out to be hopelessly romantic: There's still hope for you! Use the following notepad to write down your wishes and requests for your partner and then leave this book open on his pillow. We are sure he will take at least some of it to heart.

Darling, I would like you to

....
....
....
....
....
....
....
....
....
....
....
....
....
....
....

Chapter 5

Marriage, Love, Romance & Sex

Pairing; One Man - One Woman

Pair-bonding has been the general living concept for humans for thousands of years. It was usually an arrangement where a male kept his favourite female and, if he could afford to feed them, several other females, plus a range of indiscriminate one-off sexual encounters on the side. Modern marriage is a recent development. Whenever any human activity is surrounded by elaborate rituals and public declarations however, it is usually contrary to our biology and is intended to make people do something they would not naturally do.

This is not to say that marriage has no place in modern society, but it's important to understand its history and its relationship to our biology. But one important question remains to be answered: What is the advantage to men of marriage? In basic evolutionary terms, there is none. A man is like a rooster whose urge is to spread his genetic seed as widely as possible and as often as he can. Yet the majority of men still marry, divorced men remarry or live in pseudo-married states. This shows society's remarkable ability to restrain biologically promiscuous men.

When men walk down the aisle, many see it as the beginning of an endless supply of sex-on-demand, but this expectation, never discussed before marriage, is not how women see it. For a woman, marriage is a declaration to the world that a man regards her as 'special' and intends to have a monogamous relationship with her. Fidelity has a high priority on women's want lists, and most would be prepared to end a relationship if a man was unfaithful. This is a difference that most men never understand. Most men believe having the odd fling will not affect their relationship because men have little problem separating sex from love in the brain. For women, however, sex and love are intertwined. A sexual liaison with another woman can be seen as the ultimate betrayal, and good reason for finishing a relationship.

Sex Does Not Equal Sex

The differences between men and women could not be any greater than where sex is concerned. This has been known for thousands of years. And this fact is a major source of complaint and argument between men and women. There's an old joke that making love is what a woman does while a man is having sex with her. But that's only one of many aspects that make these differences apparent.

For example, men are always ready to have sex. Women, on the other hand, usually need an occasion and a suitable room for sex, and therefore frequently hold men's readiness against them. But men's enthusiastic and impulsive sex drive has a clear purpose – to ensure that the human species continues. And he also needs to spread his seed as far afield and as often

as possible. For a woman to feel the desire for sex, she needs to feel loved, adored and significant. Now here's the twist that most people never realise – a man needs to have sex before he can be in tune with feelings. Unfortunately, a woman needs him to do that first before she's turned on to sex. Women are often taught by their mothers that men 'just want one thing' – sex – but this is not completely accurate. Men want love, but they usually only get it through sex.

With sex, men work like gas cookers – ready in an instant – while women are like electric ovens – taking time to warm up – which often causes problems between a couple. Also, men use sex to express physically what they can't express emotionally. There are few problems a man can have that great sex won't fix. For a man to feel fulfilled through sex, he needs the release of tension. A woman has the opposite need – she needs to feel the build-up of tension over a longer period of time with her prerequisite of lots of attention and talking. He wants to empty; she wants to fill up. Understanding this difference makes men more caring lovers.

A woman, on the other hand, should show understanding when she sees a man withdraw after sex by getting up and 'doing something' such as watching TV, changing a light bulb or making coffee. This is because a man needs to feel in control of himself at all times and, during orgasm, he temporarily loses control. Getting up and doing something allows him to regain that command.

Most couples don't address these differences and each expects the other to understand their needs but that's not how nature planned it. It may be fashionable to suggest that

modern men and women are equally interested in sex, or that normal couples are perfectly matched sexually, but that's not the way it is in real life.

The sexual priorities of men and women are so opposite that it makes no sense for either to chastise the other. Neither one can help it; it's just the way they were made.

Are You Ready For Marriage?

Are you considering getting married? Or would you like to, but are not sure whether your relationship will really last? Then take the following quiz and you will find out immediately if your relationship is built on solid ground and you can plunge into the adventure of marriage without second thoughts, or whether it might be better to wait a while longer or if you should completely reconsider your decision.

Tick those of the following statements that you agree with.

1. ❑ You and your partner have many interests in common and you both consider that important.
2. ❑ You are looking forward to growing old together with your partner.
3. ❑ You have arranged your household to mutual satisfaction.
4. ❑ You laugh often when you're together.
5. ❑ After an argument each of you might make the first move toward peace.
6. ❑ Each of you still meets your own friends regularly.
7. ❑ You both have similar expectations of life.
8. ❑ You agree on whether you want children or not, and how many.
9. ❑ You always feel happy and safe with your partner.
10. ❑ You think alike where money is concerned.
11. ❑ You both have a job you like and which is equally important to each of you.
12. ❑ Your can accept your partner's few weaknesses.
13. ❑ You think very highly of your partner and show him/her your respect.
14. ❑ You know about each other's sexual desires and talk about them regularly.
15. ❑ You are sure that crises make your relationship stronger.
16. ❑ You are both equally ready for compromise.
17. ❑ You both like each other's families and care about them in the same way.
18. ❑ Your friends like your partner a lot and vice versa.
19. ❑ You are both able to admit to your faults and don't dig your heels in.
20. ❑ You trust each other.

The Unmasking of Unfaithfulness

A man who is married or in a long-term relationship is always secretly worried that single men are having more sex and more fun than him. He imagines wild singles parties, adventurous, commitment-free coupling and jacuzzis full of naked models. He fears opportunity is swinging right by him, and he's missing out completely. It doesn't matter that, when he was single, such opportunities never presented themselves anyway. He forgets about those evenings sitting alone eating cold baked beans out of a can, the humiliating rebuffs from women in front of friends at parties and the long periods without sex. He just can't help worrying that commitment equals missing out.

These worries however, are alien to women. Women are not constantly wondering about what they might miss but enjoy what they have gained. Unlike men, women who are unfaithful are not looking for great adventures or tingling erotic interludes. While there will always be exceptions to the rule, in most cases women feel neglected or not loved by their partner, so in having an affair, they look for the security and closeness they miss.

What about your partner? Is he/she really faithful? Or are there reasons to mistrust him/her? Is he/she always honest with you or does he/she have an eye on his/her own urges once in a while?

Maybe you have not known your partner for long and would like to put him/her to the test? Here's your opportunity...

Tick each question with the answer that fits your partner best. Unless specified, the word 'him' will apply equally to men and women.

1. **Is your partner jealous?**
    - ❏ Yes, very much. (A)
    - ❏ No, not at all. (C)
    - ❏ Now and then, but not excessively. (B)

2. **And what about you?**
    - ❏ Yes, very much. (A)
    - ❏ No, not at all. (C)
    - ❏ Now and then, but not excessively. (B)

3. **What does your partner think about faithfulness in general?**
    - ❏ Basically, it's very important to him, but he would probably forgive a little unfaithfulness. (C)
    - ❏ To him, being faithful is the prerequisite of a relationship. (A)
    - ❏ In his past relationships he was not too strict about it. (B)

4. **And what about you?**
    - ❏ Basically, it's very important to you, but you would forgive him a little unfaithfulness. (C)
    - ❏ To you, being faithful is the prerequisite of a relationship. (A)
    - ❏ In your past relationships you were not too strict about it. (B)

5. Has your partner ever lied to you?
- ❏ No, never. (A)
- ❏ Maybe he has used a little white lie, but you've probably done so, too. (B)
- ❏ Yes, more than once. (C)

6. How does your partner show you his affection?
- ❏ He tells you regularly that he loves you. (A)
- ❏ He rarely, if ever, says that he loves you. (C)
- ❏ Not in so many words, but more by his gestures and actions. (B)

7. Does your partner keep secrets from you?
- ❏ Not that you know of. You always tell each other everything. (A)
- ❏ Yes, and you suffer from it because you always let him in on everything. (C)
- ❏ He certainly has some, but as long as they are only small secrets, you don't mind – you have some of your own. (B)

8. Does your partner like to talk about his former partners or affairs?
- ❏ Yes, more often than you'd like him to. (C)
- ❏ No, he never does, although you would like to know more about them. (A)
- ❏ You both don't discuss it. (B)

9. Does your partner often do things without telling you where he's going or whom he's meeting?
- ❑ No, you always know where he is and with whom. (A)
- ❑ Yes, frequently, and he always becomes irritable if you ask about him it. (C)
- ❑ You don't have to know exactly where he's going and what he's doing – after all, it's the same the other way round. (B)

10. Do you know your partner's friends and acquaintances, even those of the other sex?
- ❑ As far as you know, yes. (A)
- ❑ No, only a few. (C)
- ❑ Not all but most of them – and it's the same the other way round. (B)

11. Have you ever suspected that your partner might be having an affair?
- ❑ Yes, more than once. (C)
- ❑ No, never. (A)
- ❑ You don't take that so seriously and anyway you trust each other. (B)

12. Does your partner sometimes go into raptures about film stars or other famous people?
- ❑ Yes, and he makes no secret of his enthusiasm. (C)
- ❑ No, he doesn't do things like that. (A)
- ❑ Not really – but sometimes you are taken with somebody, too. (B)

13. Does your partner frequently go on holiday without you?
- ❏ No, we want to spend the best time of the year together. (A)
- ❏ Yes, with friends, and that's very important to him. (C)
- ❏ Now and then you both go on holidays separate from each other if you can't avoid it. That's ok with both of you. (B)

14. Has your partner ever been unfaithful with you?
- ❏ Yes, unfortunately. (C)
- ❏ Not that you know of, but you're not wondering about it either. (B)
- ❏ No, certainly not. (A)

15. Do you and your partner live far from each other or is one of you away from home a lot due to his/her job?
- ❏ No. (A)
- ❏ Yes, but we both like it that way. (B)
- ❏ Yes, and our relationship suffers as a result. (C)

Are You Resistant to Pressure?

Stressed men drink alcohol and invade another country. Stressed women eat chocolate and invade shopping centres. Under pressure, women talk without thinking and men act without thinking. That's why 90% of people in jails are men and 90% of people who see therapists are women. When men and women are both under pressure it can be an emotional minefield.

The following test measures your resistance to pressure. You will find out whether you get stressed easily which needlessly puts your relationship under strain.

Tick the answers that fit you best.

1. **You are on your way to the office but have to stop by at the pharmacy beforehand to collect some medicine you ordered. An old lady enters at the same time as you, pushes to the front and then describes all her little aches and pains to the pharmacist at great length. How do you react?**
    a) You smile and grant her the little chat. It doesn't matter about the extra five minutes you have to wait. (Type A)
    b) You feel like you might explode and give vent to your anger in a biting remark before storming off. (Type C)
    c) If you are in a real hurry you interrupt them politely and explain your situation, otherwise you let the old lady have her way. (Type B)

2. **You are preparing a conference, have a long list of things to do for it and are under extreme pressure of time. Just then your mother calls and wants to know when you will be coming over to her place again. What is your reply?**
    a) You shout at her irritably for calling you at the office, when you have told her to do that in emergencies only. Before hanging up, you snap that you don't fancy visiting her after this stupid call anyway. (Type C)
    b) You talk to your mother for a few minutes – you can spare a little time. (Type A)
    c) You tell her that you are happy she called but have no time to talk right now and will call her in the evening. (Type B)

3. **It's Christmas Eve and there's no way you can avoid the crowded city centre as you still have to get a few presents. Your partner, who comes along, takes his time and rummages about in every shop while you just want to get through your list. How do you react?**
    a) After half an hour you start an argument and tell your partner that it would have been better if you had gone without him. (Type C)
    b) You let him lead you astray and so you fritter away the afternoon together before getting the presents at the last minute. (Type A)
    c) You suggest to separate and meet again at a café two hours later – this way you are both satisfied. (Type B)

4. **What happens when you are under great stress?**
   a) You become aggressive or it affects your personality. (Type C)
   b) You just don't let things bother you. (Type A)
   c) It really depends on the situation, but basically you try to find the happy medium. (Type B)

5. **Do you often feel anxious?**
   a) Yes, very often. (Type C)
   b) No, that rarely happens. (Type B)
   c) No, never. (Type A)

Evaluations

Are You Ready For Marriage?

Please count how many boxes you ticked and read the corresponding section below.

0-5 Boxes Ticked

You should reconsider getting married. Obviously you and your partner don't agree on many things. And unfortunately, with these prerequisites, the chances of a lasting marriage are low.

6-14 Boxes Ticked

Depending on which half of the scale you are in, you should be careful. We cannot recommend you get married, without reservations. There are too many open questions between you and your partner. Think about it and consider carefully if you really want him and if so, clarify all misunderstandings before you take the vows.

15-20 Boxes Ticked

We can recommend you get married. Of course there is never a 100% guarantee that everything will go well - but in your case the prerequisites and chances are very good. So act according to the proverb "Nothing ventured, nothing gained" and fling yourself into preparations. You and your partner will surely make the best of it.

The Unmasking of Faithfulness

Now count how often you chose A, B and C. Each answer is one point. Read the section below where you scored most points.

A

Your partner may definitely be counted among the faithful ones – although even with him there can never be a 100% guarantee. He obviously expects the same of you. However, he sometimes gets a bit jealous and possessive and in exceptional circumstances he might even overstep the mark.

B

You and your partner have a very similar opinion on relationships and faithfulness. You both leave the other enough freedom and are always honest and open. You are at the same level and your relationship is marked by mutual respect. What more could you want?

C

You cannot count on your partner's absolute faithfulness. When he's just fallen in love and everything's alright in the relationship, he will not be looking for someone else. But sooner or later his urge for freedom will become stronger – and then he cannot guarantee anything.

Are You Resistant to Pressure?

Men and women each trying to cope with pressure at the same time can easily cause problems in a relationship. Firstly, men stop talking and women become worried about it. Then, women start talking and men can't handle it. To help him feel better, she tries to encourage him to talk about the problem, which is the worst thing she can do. He tells her to leave him alone and retreats to another location.

Because she's under pressure, she wants to talk about her problems, which frustrates him even more. When he retreats to a quiet place, she feels rejected and unloved and calls her mother, sister or friends.

Try to take these different ways of behaviour into account next time you feel frustrated or hassled, and don't expect your partner to react the same way as you would. That's the only way you can avoid a quarrel.

Now count how often you chose type A, B and C. Each answer is one point. Read the section below where you scored most points.

Type A

Congratulations! You are highly resistant to stress and rarely let things bother you. You know how to take everything with a sense of humour and don't let long queues, unfriendly people or stress ruin your day. However, it might happen that your

partner attacks you exactly *because* you never let your reserves down and are always unflappable.

Type B

Overall you are a balanced person and always try to keep track of things. You try to avoid stressful situations from the start and most of the time this approach works out. Because you are well organised and have your day 'under control' you seldom feel hassled. If you do feel under stress, this feeling subsides after a short time because you take immediate countermeasures.

Type C

You are under constant pressure because you are easily hassled by others or by circumstances, and because you act in a hectic and chaotic way. Most of the time you try to do too many things at once and let others (friends or colleagues) load more onto you than you can cope with. Because you don't want to give up under any circumstances or admit that you have taken on too much, you are permanently stressed. This makes you easily irritable, which then leads to arguments with your partner. Try to limit your daily load to the essentials and never vent your feelings onto others.

Chapter 6

The Truth Will Out

A man taking the ultimate lie-detector test

Types of Lies

There are four basic types of lies - the White Lie, the Beneficial Lie, the Malicious Lie and the Deceptive Lie. The White Lie is part of our social fabric and stops us from emotionally hurting or insulting each other with the cold, hard, painful truth. The Beneficial Lie is used by a person who intends to help others. For example, a farmer hiding Jews from the Nazis who is asked if he's keeping any Jews in his house is seen as acting heroically when he lies. The rescue worker who pulls a child from the remains of a burning car and lies to the child that his mother and father are OK is saving the child, in the short term, from additional trauma. Doctors who lie to a patient on their deathbed to lift their spirits or prescribe fake medication, called placebos, to patients are also technically lying.

It's the Deceptive Lie that is the dangerous one because the liar intends to harm or disadvantage the victim for their own benefit. There are two main ways of deceitful lying - concealment and falsification. In concealment, the liar doesn't

actually tell a lie, they withhold information. This kind of lying is an intentional act, never an accident. Malicious lies are told either for revenge or gain. High-profile people such as actors, the wealthy and politicians are obvious targets for malicious lies for gain. Journalists who then submit those stories to trashy tabloids and magazines, knowing them to be untrue, can also benefit, just as much as their business, political and showbiz rivals.

Malicious lies, or rumour-mongering, are often used as weapons in competitive situations. Malicious liars set out to destroy the character and reputation of their victims, usually with devastating and lasting results.

A company might, for example, spread false information that its main competitor is in financial difficulties.

The most common form of lying is self-deception, which allows a person to smoke two packs of cigarettes a day while claiming to not be addicted, or convince himself that a calorie-laden dessert will not interfere with a diet.

The closer you are to a person, the harder it is to lie to them because of the emotions involved. For example, a husband will have difficulty lying to his wife if he truly loves her but would have no difficulty lying to an enemy if captured in warfare. Herein lies the key to the pathological liar – they have no emotional attachment to anyone, so all lying is easy.

Who Lies the Most?

Most women will enthusiastically claim that, without doubt, men lie far more often than women. Scientific studies and experiments show, however, that men and women tell about the same number of lies. It's the content of their lies that differs. Women tend to lie to make others feel better and men lie to make themselves look good. Women lie to keep the relationship safe and women find it most difficult to lie about their feelings. Men lie to avoid an argument, lie about their own importance and love to lie about how wild they were when they were young.

This is the main difference between male and female lies. A woman will lie that someone looks wonderful in their new outfit, even though she thinks the person looks like a sack full of potatoes. In the same circumstances, a man will keep away from the person to avoid lying and will only lie if he is forced to give his opinion. He'll say the outfit is "interesting" or "lovely", he'll tell an indirect lie like "What can I say?" or "Words fail me" or he'll simply lie that he loves it. And when a man does tell a lie, most women are good at spotting it. A man will tell you he is second-in-charge of food distribution for an international company when he actually has a delivery run with Pizza Hut.

The evidence is clear – women lie just as much as men, they simply lie differently. Because of women's super-awareness of body language and voice signals, men get caught far more often, which makes it seem like men lie more. They don't. They just keep getting caught.

The Little Test of Swindles and White Lies

Everyone lies. Most lying occurs at first meetings where everyone wants to present themselves in the best light. Most of the lies we tell are White Lies. These are told as a way of allowing us to live together without violence and aggression because often we'd prefer to hear subtle distortions of the truth rather than the cold hard facts.

When was the last time you lied? Never? We don't believe you. Think long and hard and be honest. Well, maybe you didn't actually lie, but just let someone make a wrong assumption based on what you did or didn't tell them, or just fibbed a little to avoid hurting their feelings. Maybe it was just a little white lie?

If you had told the absolute truth to every person you interacted with over the last week, where would you be right now? In hospital? Perhaps jail? If you'd spoken the exact words going through your mind as you were thinking them, how would people have responded? One thing's for sure: you'd have no friends by now and you'd probably end up unemployed.

But what about you and the truth? Do you sometimes let yourself be carried away into using a white lie – for convenience, not to hurt anybody or to put yourself into a better light? Or do you take the truth very seriously and believe you should always tell everyone the complete truth? To find out, tick those of the following statements with which you agree. With questions that are clearly directed at the opposite sex, decide how you would behave if you were in their shoes, and then tick the appropriate box.

1. ❏ Sometimes you grin and bear it if you think it might be to your advantage.
2. ❏ You comb your last strands of hair over your bald patches and hope you can fake a full head of hair.
3. ❏ You have feigned a headache or migraine so that you could cancel an appointment or avoid sex.
4. ❏ If you are late you are never at a loss for a convincing excuse.
5. ❏ If you argue with your partner, you sometimes distort the facts to strengthen your position.
6. ❏ In reply to the question "How are you feeling?" you have replied "Great, thanks" while actually the opposite was true, but you didn't want to talk about it.
7. ❏ As a child you recited a poem on Mother's Day that praised your mother as perfect while you often thought she treated you unfairly or misunderstood you.
8. ❏ You like to wear high heels occasionally to make your legs look longer.
9. ❏ If you are asked for your age, you neatly evade an answer or give a younger age.
10. ❏ You have exaggerated a little during a job interview to present yourself in a better light.
11. ❏ When your best friend asked you what you thought about his/her new partner you said something nice although you did not really like him/her.
12. ❏ You dye your hair regularly or tint it to cover grey streaks and look younger.

13. ❏ If you wanted to sell your car you might just forget to mention that the engine sometimes loses oil.
14. ❏ If your aunt gives you a hideous vase as a birthday present, you say "How nice" because you don't want to hurt her.
15. ❏ When you are invited for dinner you always say that you liked the food (even if you didn't) just to please the cook.
16. ❏ If you chat on the internet you are not very accurate about your personal details.
17. ❏ When an acquaintance showed you their new outfit you said, "Suits you perfectly" although you considered it revolting.
18. ❏ You have told a child that Father Christmas or the Easter Bunny really exist.
19. ❏ You frequently use make-up and have also thought about or used artificial fingernails.
20. ❏ If you put your house on the market you may not mention right away that it is in the approach path to the airport.

The Ultimate Lie Detector Test

We lie for two reasons – to make a gain or avoid a pain. Fortunately, most people feel a sense of guilt, remorse or unease when they lie, and most find it impossible to hide. It then becomes possible for the other person to work out whether they're being told the truth – or are being lied to. With a little practice, you can learn to recognise these behavioural signals, and know how to decode them. (Read *The Definitive Book of Body Language* by Allan & Barbara Pease).

However, there is no infallible lie detector test that is absolutely watertight every time. Experienced liars usually show little tension and are more likely to pass the test than honest people who are always nervous in exam situations. That's why the questions and tasks below can only offer the clues that can help you unmask a liar.

If your partner is a woman, read part 1 of this test, if he's a man, read part 2 carefully. If you are gay, answer as if your partner's behaviour is more masculine or feminine than yours. In every case, tick all statements that fit your partner in the situations described or in similar situations. It's also possible to tick none or more than one answer per question.

Part 1

For men only to answer

1. When you open the shoe cupboard or the area where your partner's shoes take up three quarters of the space anyway, an unworn pair of shoes falls out, that you haven't seen before. Obviously your partner has been shopping again. What does she say when you mention it?
   - ❏ She says: "Oh yes, those shoes. I completely forgot to tell you about them. Aren't they nice" and she smiles self-consciously.
   - ❏ She brushes the matter aside and hums and haws: "Oh those, . . . I . . . um . . . bought them ages ago . . . but just never got to wear them."
   - ❏ She seems completely unnerved and says, with a slightly aggressive undertone: "I borrowed them from Sue. Don't you believe me?"
   - ❏ "Ooh, I wonder where these came from?" she says, feigning a sudden attack of amnesia before she wanders off mumbling, "No idea".
   - ❏ "They were very cheap. A real bargain, take my word for it", she claims in a higher pitched voice that usual.

2. **For some time you've been suspicious that your partner is not playing tennis with her best friend when she claims to be. Although you have no reason to think she's having an affair, you can feel that something's wrong. One evening you take her to task and ask her – factually but directly – about it. What happens?**
   - ❑ She appears scandalized: "I swear, I'm playing tennis with Sarah." However, her voice is trembling slightly.
   - ❑ She demands indignantly that you immediately call her friend and hear for yourself that she's completely honest with you. She even hands you the telephone. But one of her eyes is twitching.
   - ❑ She rubs her hand nervously but claims that she's definitely been playing tennis. She even adds: "How can you accuse me like that?"
   - ❑ She seems completely astonished and says surprisedly: "I have no reason to lie to you." However, she avoids further questions by claiming that she really does not have to get involved in a ridiculous conversation like this.
   - ❑ She is beside herself with rage and accuses you of driving her into someone else's arms with your stupid jealousy. While she's saying this, the corner of her mouth twitches and her pupils contract slightly.

3. You would like to subject your car to an extensive clean up and are looking for the old pair of jeans you have kept for occasions like this. Although you have been looking all over the place, you still haven't found them. At a loss, you ask your partner if she knows where your jeans are. How does she react?

- ❏ She becomes indignant and shouts at you cheekily: "Is it my fault that you can't keep an organised clothes cupboard? It's really not my problem if you can't find your rags" before rushing from the room.
- ❏ She flushes and turns away, before mumbling barely audible: "I haven't got the slightest idea. Honestly!"
- ❏ "Maybe ... they are ... in ... in the wash", she stammers, sighs slightly and proposes in a pronouncedly friendly way: "Why don't you wear the brown cargo trousers instead?"
- ❏ "Don't know," she says and turns away hastily. "I'll help you look for them," she offers – something she has never done before.
- ❏ She says: "Oh, those ... well, um ... I put them in the tumble dryer the other day and they shrunk. So unfortunately I had to throw them out. I'm really sorry! I would have told you earlier but ... " Or she's says something toxic spilled on them and she had to throw them out.

4. **You bought a flat together with your partner and you both agreed to make sacrifices. You unyieldingly stick to the plan, even if you find it difficult, while your partner has once again come home with a new piece of designer clothing. How does she justify her purchase?**

- ❑ She claims that her best friend gave her the cardigan as a present to make her happy, and intently watches her fingernails.
- ❑ Without any trace of a bad conscience but several tones higher than normal she says: "Darling, you don't really want an argument now, do you?"
- ❑ She deliberately ignores your question and asks in return: "I had to buy it. Or would you like me to go to the office in the nude?"
- ❑ She grins self-consciously and tries to flatter you: "I'll look so sexy in it that every man will be jealous of you at that party tomorrow night."
- ❑ She rubs her nose with an embarrassed look and says: "It was a bargain . . . on sale! And we even saved more money, because Emma was buying one, which made mine even cheaper."

GABS.

5. You mother has invited you and your partner for lunch on Sunday. Your mother is easily displeased if somebody's late. Your partner visits a friend in the morning but promises to be back in plenty of time – which, of course, is not the case. What is her excuse?
   - ❏ She starts to recount the morning in tiny detail, dramatising each event drastically but does not give a reason for her being late.
   - ❏ She fumbles the zipper of her coat and says: "It's Amy's fault. She held me back. Honestly. You can ask her if you don't believe me."
   - ❏ She says in a much louder voice than normally: "I'm sorry. The car didn't start and the phone battery was flat."
   - ❏ She only says: "It's not my fault. You have to believe me."
   - ❏ She tries to distract you by saying that your mother is a pain-in-the-arse and that her exaggerated punctuality gets on her nerves.

Part 2

Ladies only

1. Your partner comes home at four in the morning, slightly off balance. He was at a friend's house for a 'sociable evening'. He smells conspicuously of peppermint (which he doesn't even like) and tries to be quiet and not to wake you. You immediately take him to task and ask reproachfully whether he's drunk. How does he react?
   - ❏ He mumbles: "Naaaaa, I'm nott drunnkatall."
   - ❏ He tells you about the evening in as unconcerned a voice as possible but talks much louder and faster than usual.
   - ❏ He only says: "I didn't drink much. Honestly!"
   - ❏ He denies it, but obviously avoids your gaze.
   - ❏ He replies: "I'm sober. May lightning strike me if I'm not telling the truth!"

2. You wanted to go to a concert after work with a colleague. She cancels at the last minute and therefore you get home before your partner does. On the answering machine there is a message from a Charlotte (whom you don't know) asking, in a purring voice, "darling ... please call me ... " What happens when you take him to task later?

   ❑ "Who's that supposed to be?" he warbles. "I don't know this person."
   ❑ He says: "No idea, darling. She must have dialled the wrong number", while rummaging through his briefcase.
   ❑ "Must be a bad joke" he tries to explain without looking at you.
   ❑ "Can't a man have some rest after a long day at work?" he asks aggressively as if to strike back. "I really don't feel like coping with your ridiculous insinuations right now."
   ❑ "It's nothing to do with me", he says and looks at you with puppy eyes. "I swear on my mother's grave."

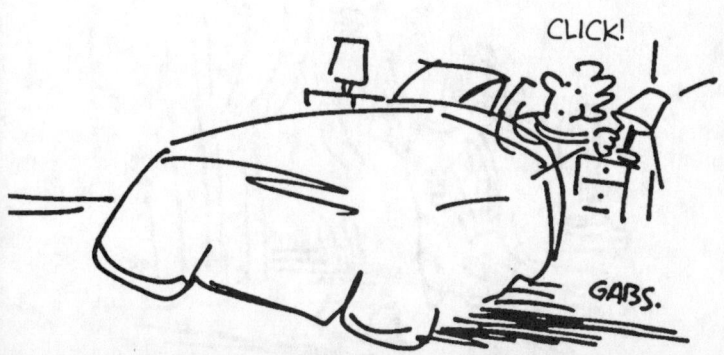

3. You've planned a night at the opera for a long time and asked your partner to buy the tickets. As you want to go to the premiere, immediate action to buy the tickets is needed. When you ask him about the tickets three days later, it turns out that the show is sold out – and that you don't have tickets after all. Disappointedly, you ask him why he didn't buy them in time. What happens?
   - ❏ He becomes indignant and starts shouting at you. He reacts with unexpected fervour and can hardly be calmed down. He then says that he doesn't feel like going anywhere with you, anyway.
   - ❏ He tells you an involved but outrageous story to justify his actions that contains the phrase "You've gotta believe me" at least three times.
   - ❏ He tells you a long-winded story about his failed attempts at getting the tickets, wipes his eyes repeatedly and constantly rubs the tip of his nose.
   - ❏ He smiles slowly, as if in agony, and claims the show had already been sold out for a long time when you asked him to get tickets.
   - ❏ He tries to distract you but his face has become red and flushed.

4. **It's your wedding anniversary. Your partner has to leave the house very early because of a business appointment so you don't see each other before the evening when he comes back from the office. At first, you leave your present in a drawer and wait to see what happens. When he starts reading the paper, you are certain that he's forgotten about the anniversary. You ask him carefully about it, without reproaching or blaming him. What does he do?**
    - ❏ He claims he left your present in the car, goes outside and returns ten minutes later with a bunch of flowers from the petrol station and a forgiving grin on his face.
    - ❏ He says with conviction, but in a much higher voice than usual: "Darling, we really don't have to prove our love with material things, do we?"
    - ❏ He explains that it's all his secretary's fault and puts his hands in his pockets.
    - ❏ He starts running up and down the house and repeatedly claims to have hidden the present somewhere but is not able to find it right now. The next day he presents you with a gift that – by pure coincidence – he found in the morning.
    - ❏ He stammers for a few minutes without being able to explain what happened and says "um" and "hum" and "well" all the time, which is normally not his way of talking.

5. You and your partner have been invited to a New Year's party at a friend's house. It's semi-formal and you want to look good under any circumstances. After having tried on nearly all the contents of your wardrobe you end up wearing the first dress you took out. You ask your partner how you look. What is his reply?
    - ❑ "Wonderful, darling", without having looked at you even once.
    - ❑ He fumbles his tie a few times although it fits perfectly and mumbles barely audibly: "We're late. Everything's fine. We really have to go."
    - ❑ "You know that to me you always look beautiful" he claims, trying to sound as sincere as possible.
    - ❑ "Beautiful. Why should I lie to you? You know I would never do that."
    - ❑ "Just wonderful", he says and hurries from the room.

Evaluations

 The Little Test of Swindles and White Lies

Please count how many boxes you ticked and read the corresponding section below.

0–5 Boxes Ticked

You are amazing! You seem to be immune even against little every-day lies. If you answered the questions in this test honestly – and we presume you did – you are a real phenomenon – or a poor sap.

Why? If you go through life under the motto: "I could never lie to anyone" and always tell everybody the truth, you don't do yourself or anyone else a real favour. Remember that most people don't like to look truth in the eye. People say they love the truth but, in reality, they want to believe that which they love is true.

6–14 Boxes Ticked

You're about average. You don't lie consciously or with deliberate intent, but you've used one trick or another from time to time to make yourself look better, in order not to attract attention or to do someone a favour.

As long as you make sure you don't use white lies too often and get tangled in a web of deceit that you can't get away from without harm, everything's alright.

15–20 Boxes Ticked

If lies were put to music, you'd be a symphony orchestra! White lies are your standard form of communication and are used according to your needs. But even if you are convinced by your ability to deceive others you should be careful. Especially if you used to lie to your parents to avoid punishment when you were a child and now you don't even recoil from solid lies and fraudulence.

Most lies can be detected because they usually involve emotions that leak out as body language and verbal red lights. The bigger the lie and the more emotions involved, the more clues will leak out from the liar.

The Ultimate Lie Detector Test

No matter whether your partner is male or female or whether you answered Part One or Two of our test, if you ticked more than one box for one question, you can be almost certain that your partner is lying to you.

If you frequently have suspicions or if a number of the described situations fit your partner, you should urgently discuss this with him or her.

Keep in mind that some of the signals that are mentioned here show a person is experiencing some kind of stress and are not guarantees that they are lying. There are also a small percentage of people who are comfortable about lying and don't show many stress-related signals, whereas others such as political or religious fanatics, can actually believe their own lies and therefore don't display any signs of deceit. But most liars display many signs, most of the time.

There is a reason why women are better at detecting lies than men:

MRI brain scans reveal the average woman has between 14 and 16 key locations working in both brain hemispheres when she is communicating face-to-face. These locations are used to decode words, tone of voice changes and body signals, and largely account for what is known as 'a woman's intuition'. A male typically has only 4 to 7 of these locations because male brains have evolved more for spatial tasks than communication skills.

This gives women the additional advantage of being able to read body signals and listen to what is being said while, at the same time, talking. Males, with their mono-tracking brains, focus on one piece of information at a time and consequently miss many of the body signals.

Chapter 7

The Other Woman - His Mother

It wasn't until their wedding night that Fiona realised Michael, age 36, still let his mother buy his underwear...

Enter, the Dragon

Mothers-in-law probably inspire more jokes than any other group of people on earth. They are constantly the butt of humour by comedians, between men and in TV sitcoms. They are consistently characterised as witches, battleaxes or shrews. One of the founders of modern Russia, Lenin, when asked what should be the maximum penalty for bigamy, replied: "Two mothers-in-law".

Mothers-in-law do cause a problem in many people's marriages, with up to a third who break up blaming the mother-in-law for the rift. But not all mothers-in-law live up to the dreaded reputation of wickedness. Half of them are either neutral at worst, or they can also be loving, helpful and generous members of the extended family. And mothers-in-law are often blamed for the shortcomings and emotional problems of their sons or daughters-in-law.

However, it's not usually the woman's mother who causes most of the problems. Research shows time and time again, that it's usually the man's mother who is the real danger. His

mother-in-law may provoke the most public complaints, but these are usually more tongue-in-cheek than protesting about a real problem. A man's mother-in-law might irritate him, nag him and exasperate him, but most men don't usually dislike them. Mother-in-law problems don't dominate men's lives.

There's an old Polish proverb: "The way to a mother-in-law's heart is through her daughter." Most men realise this. What most women's mothers want, more than anything, is to see their daughters happy. And if the men in their lives make them happy, they're unlikely to cause problems. If they're going to have problems with their in-laws, it's far more likely to come from their father-in-law refusing to let go of his cherished 'princess'.

It's likely that the quizzes in this chapter will have strong appeal to women – especially as men don't tend to worry as much about their mothers-in-law. Men should still read the quizzes and consider all the evaluations, as they contain valuable information that can help to clarify things. However, there is one quiz we have devised especially for men, to make them more aware of possible problems between their partner and their mother.

Warming Yourself Up

Here we have collected the best jokes about mothers-in-law to put you in a humorous frame of mind for the following tests. Just choose the one you like best, compare it to your partner's choice and have a good laugh before turning to the more serious side of this topic.

What's the difference between a Rottweiler and a mother-in-law? Eventually, the Rottweiler lets go.

My mother-in-law called by this morning. When I answered the door she asked, "Can I stay here for a few days?"
"You certainly can," I replied... and I closed the door.

Adam and Eve were the happiest and luckiest couple in the world, because neither of them had a mother-in-law.

How many mothers-in-law does it take to change a light bulb?
One. She just holds it up and waits for the world to revolve around her.

A man was asked: "Why are you at the office today? Shouldn't you be attending your mother-in-law's funeral?"
"Yes," he replied, "But business before pleasure."

If you could convince your mother-in-law to walk 10 kilometres a day, after just one week she'd be 70 miles away.

My mother-in-law and I were happy for 20 years. Then we met.

I received an email today advising that my mother-in-law had passed away and asking whether to arrange a burial, a cremation or embalming. I replied, "Be absolutely sure – arrange all three."

The Great Endurance Test

Do you and your partner often argue because of his or your mother? With this test you can find out how much of a burden your mother-in-law is – or isn't – for your relationship. Tick the boxes in front of the following statements which you agree with.

1. ❑ My mother-in-law mothered and pampered my partner all his life. She cooked, cleaned, washed and ironed for him. Now he expects me to do the same and his mother supports his attitude.
2. ❑ My mother-in-law often interferes with our relationship and always takes her son's side.
3. ❑ I'm glad when we're going on holiday because I won't see my mother-in-law for two whole weeks.
4. ❑ My partner is more relaxed on holidays and we argue much less than when we are at home.
5. ❑ I have repeatedly accused my partner that his relationship with his mother is too close and that he takes too much from her.
6. ❑ It's always such a relief when Christmas is over, because my mother-in-law is leaving again.
7. ❑ My mother-in-law spoils my children and often ignores my instructions not to slip them sweets or junk food.
8. ❑ My mother-in-law does not understand that my partner and I need time to ourselves once in a while and she feels easily neglected.
9. ❑ I often feel uneasy and insecure when my mother-in-law is present. I feel like I'm under constant surveillance.

10. ❑ My mother-in-law insists on us coming for lunch every Sunday. She always makes my partner's favourite food so that "the boy gets a decent meal for a change".
11. ❑ My mother-in-law calls us often and asks my partner constantly when he's coming over to mow the lawn, to paint the house or to do other work for her.
12. ❑ My mother-in-law makes constant demands.
13. ❑ My mother-in-law criticizes me all the time and emphasises again and again that she does things differently, no matter whether it's about cooking, work in the house or our children's education.
14. ❑ In my opinion, my mother-in-law demands far too much attention from my partner.
15. ❑ My mother-in-law is very nosy. She constantly wants to know the most intimate details about our marriage.
16. ❑ My mother-in-law doesn't believe I'm capable of much and always gives me advice without being asked for it.
17. ❑ My mother-in-law expects my partner to obey her as if he were still a small boy and gets annoyed if he does not comply.
18. ❑ My mother-in-law wants to be in on everything in our lives and feels easily excluded.
19. ❑ My mother-in-law drops in uninvited and unannounced because, as she always puts it, "she is family".
20. ❑ I have already thought about leaving my partner because of his mother.

The Ultimate Mother-in-Law Test

What about your mother-in-law then? Are you lucky and get along well with her? Or does she always interfere and make your life hell? This quiz helps you to clarify what kind of person your mother-in-law is: a merciless old battleaxe or motherly friend, dominant egoist or relentless moaner – the following test will tell you. Tick the statements that best fit your mother-in-law. For each question tick one answer only.

Quiz 1 – (For women to answer)

Your partner and his mother

1. It's your partner's birthday soon and you plan a little party for him. As your in-laws live in the same city you invite them, too. What happens?
    a) Your mother-in-law drops in uninvited a few days before the party to talk you through a few details. She offers to come over early and help with the preparations. She wants to make dessert – nothing can dissuade her. And she does not let up until you tell her what you are giving him as a present. (Type C)
    b) When you invite your mother-in-law to the party, the first thing she wants to know is what's for dinner. She then makes suggestions for changes of the menu. After all, she knows best what your partner likes, she's known him much longer than you. She comments on the list of guests as always and wants to know why you didn't invite dear old Aunt Agatha, which by the way, she thinks is far from acceptable. (Type B)
    c) Your mother-in-law is offended because you haven't told her about the party beforehand. She would have liked to organise a dinner herself and now feels left out. She accuses you of having acted on your own authority. Afterwards she complains about you to your partner and tries to change his mind about the party. (Type A)
    d) A few days before the party your mother-in-law calls to thank you for the invitation. After a little chat, she says good-bye, because she has things to do. Before hanging up she mentions that she would love to help you out if you need her for anything. (Type D)

2. It's only a short time before Christmas. You and your partner decided to spend the holidays on your own. You will neither visit nor invite your or his parents, both of whom live 150 kilometres away. When your mother-in-law learns about your plan...

   a) ... she acts out a nervous breakdown on the phone with a performance that should be awarded an Oscar. She accuses your partner of breaking the family tradition and says she has no intention to accept that. And she accuses you of estranging the family. She starts to shout and finally gives you an ultimatum. (Type A)

   b) ... she immediately wants to know why you don't want to come and what you will be doing instead. When she hears that your parents will have to do without you, too, she is at least partly reconciled. Nevertheless, she calls a few times during the following days and tells you about her friends who will all be visited by their children. (Type B)

   c) ... she's happy for you and hopes you have a nice day. She has decided to break with Christmas traditions and has secretly booked a trip for her husband and herself. (Type D)

   d) ... she tells you how much she regrets that you are not coming but accepts it and does not try to persuade you to change your mind. Nevertheless, she'll call at least three times on Christmas Day and sends you a huge package of stuff to remind your partner of Christmas at home. (Type C)

3. **You and your partner want to get married. You give your in-laws the happy news. Which of the following sentences sounds like your mother-in-law?**
    a) Congratulations! I'm so happy for you. (Type D)
    b) Don't you think it's a bit early for that? (Type A)
    c) Make sure you treat my darling well! (Type B)
    d) Welcome to my family. I hope we will get along well. (Type C)

4. **You and your partner are expecting a baby in three months' time. Together, you discuss maternity and paternity leave and what the child's daily routine will be. How does your mother-in-law behave?**
   a) She keeps telling you that she would be more than willing to take care of the baby in case you both want to return to your jobs soon after the child's birth. Besides, she spends more time at your place than at her own home and can hardly be kept from coming along when you go to your gynaecologist or look for a pram. She even wants to be there during the birth. (Type C)
   b) She brings in loads of books about the topic and interferes all the time with your discussions. Without being asked, she relates her own and her friends' experiences, has an argument against everything you say and warns you of separating the child too early from his/her mother. (Type B)
   c) If you ask her, she tells you what in her opinion the advantages and disadvantages are. Apart from that, she thinks it's your decision. Nevertheless you know that you can rely on her – no matter what your decision might be. (Type D)
   d) First she instructs you on how it used to be in her time and tells you without any doubt that mother and child belong together. The man is the breadwinner, that's the way things should be. (Type A)

5. **Your child has been born by now and you are still trying to cope with the new situation. What does your mother-in-law do?**
   a) She keeps asking about her grandchild and gives you loads of advice for the first few weeks. She emphasises all the time how much you can do during this important phase and knows a story for every possible situation. (Type B)
   b) She likes to come over when she's invited and always makes sure beforehand, whether you are OK with her dropping in. She often brings something along and lends you a hand when things are in turmoil. (Type D)
   c) She calls every day to ask about you and the baby's well-being and when she can come and visit her grandchild again. When she's there she often stays longer than planned because she can't tear herself away from the child. She also wants to know all the details about the birth. (Type C)
   d) She nags about everything you do. In extreme cases she complains about you and even insults you. As soon as your partner takes her to task for it, she denies everything and accuses you of wanting to drive a wedge between her and her son. (Type A)

6. How did your mother-in-law behave when you first met her?
   a) She came over to you at once, talked to you as if you were old friends and told you the whole story of her life. (Type C)
   b) She pestered the living daylights out of you with her questions and explained to you how your partner "works". (Type B)
   c) After a warm welcome you got into a nice conversation and spent a few great hours together. (Type D)
   d) She asked you all sorts of personal questions and after half an hour gave advice for every problem you had. (Type A)

Part 2 (For men to answer)

Your Mother and your wife/partner - How Well Do They Get Along?

Do your partner and your mother get along well? Or is there often a bad atmosphere because they hold different opinions? Is the trouble really always your partner's fault, as your mother sometimes claims? Or does she also contribute to it? And is everything still running smoothly with you and your partner or is there an urgent need for action if you don't want to put your relationship at risk? This quiz gives you the answers.

Tick the boxes in front of the following statements which you agree with.

1. ❑ Your mother has frequently said one of the following things to you:
    "After all I've done for you!"
    "Who else do I have to turn to?"
    "You don't care about me any more."
    "When I'm dead and gone, you'll be sorry."
    "You're selfish – just like your father."
    "I feel so alone now."
2. ❑ Each time she has evoked feelings of guilt with you, you started to defend your mother against your partner.
3. ❑ You consider it your duty to take care of your mother but your partner does not seem to care, as she has emphasised more than once that your mother takes up too much space in your life.
4. ❑ You partner does not understand why you frequently do repairs or other little tasks for your mother.

5. ❑ Your mother complains to you or others that your partner excludes her.
6. ❑ Your mother wants to give your partner precious advice but your partner feels patronised and dismisses it.
7. ❑ Both women compete jealously about your children and have opposing opinions about most matters of education.
8. ❑ You don't understand why everybody is furious all the time while you just try to get along well with everybody.
9. ❑ Your mother still likes to treat you to your favourite meal, which makes your partner fume with rage. But your mother's roast is just simply the best.
10. ❑ When your partner wants to talk to you about your mother you frequently stall because you think your partner exaggerates too much.
11. ❑ In contrast to your partner, you don't have problems with your mother coming over without prior notice. After all, you have nothing to hide.
12. ❑ Your partner frequently feels controlled by your mother who only shows a lively interest in your life.
13. ❑ At first your partner and your mother got along well. Only when you moved in together did the relationship turn sour – and you simply cannot understand why.
14. ❑ Your mother keeps complaining that your partner trusts her own mother more than her.
15. ❑ Sometimes you get the impression that the women are competing about you.

Evaluations

 **The Great Endurance Test**

Please count how many boxes you ticked and read the corresponding section below.

0–5 Boxes Ticked

You really can't complain about your mother-in-law. She puts hardly any strain on your relationship. Obviously you succeeded in building up a good relationship with your partner's mother and integrate her adequately into your own relationship. The three of you are emotionally well balanced, independent, unselfish and caring and your behaviour is motivated by neither jealousy, possessiveness, dependence, immaturity, selfishness or emotional instability. But don't forget to set boundaries now and then, even if your mother-in-law's help and advice are often welcome. It's the only way to keep up the good relationship.

6–14 Boxes Ticked

The relationship with your mother-in-law is not seriously strained but she is often the cause of unpleasant discussions between you and your partner. Keep in mind that sons rarely talk with their mothers about much. Consequently, a mother-in-law will seldom get much information and begins to feel excluded from her son's new family and may think the only

way she can be included is to force her way by being constantly present.

Maybe you should try to be a bit more diplomatic in the future and integrate your mother-in-law a little more. This way, she will feel relieved and withdraw by herself.

The last thing a woman needs is a mother-in-law complaining about her to her husband; she really needs an ally as opposed to an enemy. Therefore, you have to be the one to try and build bridges, because if you invest no time at all in the relationship with your mother-in-law, there will be a negative dividend.

15–20 Boxes Ticked

Your relationship is under considerable strain. You have a meddling, possessive and intrusive mother-in-law who won't cut the umbilical cord with her son. Some days your mother-in-law crisis seems so unmanageable and causes so much misery that you even think about divorce. But you still have to make your lives work. As women, you need to sort this relationship out between yourselves without getting your husband/son involved. You need to take control of the situation. Instead of criticising his mother, it's far more effective to train him to do what you want him to do, and stop blaming her. He's now an adult and must be responsible for his own actions.

The Ultimate Mother-in-Law Test

Please count how often you chose type A, B, C and D. Each answer is one point. Read the section below where you got most points.

Type A

You don't have an easy life! Your mother-in-law is overbearing. She always gets her way, everybody lets her have her way for the sake of peace and everybody does as she says. Whenever you voice an opinion that doesn't coincide with hers, an argument always develops. She gets very touchy about any opposition. After all, she believes that she's the only one who really knows what's right or wrong where her child (your partner) is concerned.

Consequently, she does not mince her words when it's about telling you what you should change and does not refrain from criticism and expressing her displeasure. This type of person is difficult to deal with as she will immediately feel unfairly treated if you show any signs of opposing her. She clearly sees her child's partner as an opponent and, because of her fear of loss, she will try to hold and defend her position.

Therefore, not only do you have to tread carefully around her, but you also need a lot of patience. Unfortunately, it will always be difficult to maintain a relaxed relationship with her.

Type B

Your mother-in-law means well and is usually a polite and obliging person, but she is also very dominant and interferes more with your life than you feel is acceptable. She knows everything, comments on everything and is moralistic, although she always gives her advice in a friendly tone. Unfortunately, she always wants to interfere and tries to influence your daily lives, from educating your children, choosing a place to go on holiday or household matters such as the correct way to stack a dishwasher or clean a floor – she has to be part of everything. This is the only way for her to keep control – and that is her ultimate aim.

She wants to be in on everything and never minds her own business, disguising her nosiness as concern for the family. Basically, you can get along fine with this kind of mother-in-law as long as you let her have it her way. From her standpoint, she doesn't consider you an opponent but only wants what is best for her child.

Type C

Your mother-in-law is a warm and friendly person. She seems to be sympathetic, altruistic and near perfect – you simply can't help but like her. She treats the friends and partners of her children as if they have always been part of the family and has received you warmly as well.

She is very good to everybody around her and anticipates your and your partner's every wish. If you need help, she's always there.

She easily trusted you and tells you the most intimate things from her life. But there is a hidden trade-off expected by this kind of person. She easily oversteps her boundaries and expects the same from you – to tell her intimate details about your relationship.

She has a very close relationship with her children and behaves like their good friend but she sometimes forgets one thing: She is your partner's mother and should try and keep a healthy distance for your relationship's sake.

Type D
Congratulations! You have clearly the best of all mothers-in-law. She is sympathetic, uncomplicated, open, tolerant, generous, friendly but still unobtrusive – she's almost perfect. You liked each other from the start and can talk about anything. You have a friendly relationship with her and sometimes even feel close to her – but not too close or restricted.

Your mother-in-law respects your privacy and sets boundaries herself. After all, she uses the freedom she gained when her children left home. She is able to let go and let her children have a life of their own – with all its consequences. All this adds up to a friendly and relaxed relationship full of mutual respect for each person.

Mother and Daughter-in-Law – How Well Do They Get Along?

Count how many boxes you ticked and read the corresponding section below.

0–3 Boxes Ticked

You don't have to worry about your relationship. Your partner and your mother get along well or very well. And even if they disagree now and then, they are certainly capable of solving their problems without your help. There is no need for you to take action on any issue.

4–10 Boxes Ticked

Even if you don't want to deal with it, the relationship between your partner and your mother is not always the best. Those two women disagree on many things and often get into a fight. Try to take an objective view on the matter and support your partner. After all, you're living with her, not with your mother.

11–15 Boxes Ticked

Your partner is at loggerheads with your mother. There's no way you could miss or ignore that. Get together with both of them and try to talk reasonably. Bring up their mutual problems

and try to find solutions together. If this is not possible, make clear arrangements with your partner to include your mother only in certain matters (but then do it consciously), encourage your mother to develop activities of her own and deny her some things. Learn how to set boundaries – in a polite way. Your relationship should be worth it as this is the only way you can lead a happy and independent life.

Chapter 8

Language problems

Men were never great conversationalists

The Basic Rules of Communication

In Chapter 1 we covered the problems of talking and listening. In this chapter we will answer the question, 'Why do men and women have so many problems communicating with each other?'

One principle needs to be made clear right from the beginning: men are problem-solvers and women are nest-builders.

The mysterious world of women's language still amuses and irritates most men and the following five questions on female communicative behaviour are the ones that men wonder about most:

1. Why do women talk so much?
2. Why do women always want to talk about problems?
3. Why do women exaggerate?
4. Why do women never seem to get to the point?
5. Why do women always want to know all the little details?

Women, on the other hand, often despair about male communication and ask themselves:

1. Why are men so direct?
2. Why do you always have to drag everything out of men?
3. Why are men so often silent?
4. Why do men never want to know any details?
5. Why do men always give unsolicited advice?

There are a number of reasons for each of these behaviours that we can't address in detail here, but if you bear the following rules in mind, nothing (or at least not much) should hinder a smooth communication between you and your partner.

Rules For Women to Communicate with Men

- Keep everything as simple as possible.
- Never talk about more than one thing at a time.
- Use short, clear sentences and limit yourself to the essentials.
- Use direct talk – say exactly what you want.
- Do not interrupt him when he speaks.
- Inform him what you would like to talk about, or if you want to discuss a serious problem!
- Never stay silent in order to punish him. Men love silence – it's a bonus.

Rules For Men to Communicate with Women

- Simply listen; make typical sounds and use facial expressions.
- Refrain from offering solutions.
- Express your wishes indirectly and always say 'please'!
- Don't take every word she says at face value!
- It's not the contents of what you say that count but your interest in her conversation.
- Never tell her that she dramatises things and don't correct her in front of others.
- Always give her more details than you would to a man.

The Great Test of Communication

How well do you communicate with your partner? Or do you mainly talk at cross-purposes? The following test gives you the answer in black and white. You will also get exciting insights into assessing yourself and others.

Below you will find two identical questionnaires – one for the tested person (first questionnaire) and one for the partner (second questionnaire). First you answer *your* questions, then ask your partner to fill in his/hers. In the interests of accuracy, don't discuss your answers with him/her and remember, no cheating!

If you want to test each other, copy both questionnaires before filling them in so each of you can answer the questions at the same time.

Name of tested person _____

Name of partner _____

1. **Which talking topics are most important to you? (Give three answers)**

   ....
   ....
   ....

2. **What have you and your partner been talking about today – apart from everyday matters?**

   ....

3. **If you were granted three wishes, what would they be?**

   ....
   ....
   ....

4. **Do you think you can talk well with your partner?**

   ....

5. **Do you feel understood and supported enough by your partner if you have any problems?**

   ....

6. How do you behave if your partner has problems?

   ....

7. In similar situations, what do you expect of your partner?

   ....

8. Do you think you are a good listener?

   ....

9. Do you think that your partner considers you a good listener?

   ....

10. Do you always have an open ear for your partner's wishes and worries?

    ....

11. Can you be silent together with your partner or do you find silent moments uncomfortable?

    ....

12. In discussions with your partner, do you often drag up points of dispute from past arguments?

    ....

13. If so, what do you hope might come of it?

    ....

14. Do you have to thrash out arguments before you can sleep peacefully?

    ....

15. Do you think your partner's need to talk is similar to your own?

....

16. Are you grumpy in the mornings, wanting to hide behind the newspaper, or can you chat away easily?

....

17. Are you satisfied with the communication between you and your partner?

....

Name of tested person _____

Name of partner _____

1. Which topics are most important to your partner? (Give three answers)

   ....
   ....
   ....

2. What have you and your partner been talking about today – apart from everyday matters?

   ....

3. If your partner was granted three wishes, what would they be?

   ....
   ....
   ....

4. Does your partner think he/she can talk well with you?

   ....

5. Does your partner feel understood and supported enough by you if he/she has any problems?

   ....

6. How does your partner behave if he/she has problems?

   ....

7. What does he/she expect of you in such situations?

   ....

8. Do you think that your partner is a good listener?

   ....

9. Does your partner consider you a good listener?

   ....

10. Does your partner always have an open ear for your wishes and worries?

    ....

11. Can your partner be silent together with you or does he/she find these moments uncomfortable?

    ....

12. In discussions with you, does your partner often drag up points of dispute from past arguments?

    ....

13. If so, what do you think he/she hopes might come of it?

    ....

14. Does your partner have to thrash out arguments before he/she can sleep peacefully?

    ....

15. Do you think your partner's need to talk is similar to yours?

....

16. Is your partner grumpy in the mornings, wanting to hide behind the newspaper, or can he/she chat away easily?

....

17. Is your partner satisfied with the communication between you and him/her?

....

The Art of Giving the Right Answer

This test is mainly meant for men. In communication between men and women there are often many problem areas, especially when it's about giving the right answers to tricky questions. If you're a man, you're probably tired of being accused day in and day out of never listening, never being interested in your partner's problems and always criticising her. The following test will open your eyes and help you recognise the pitfalls of female communication – and how to avoid them.

Here's how it works: below you'll find three different situations where a woman asks her partner a tricky question that, if answered wrongly, might lead to a catastrophe. Of the three possible answers or reactions, there is always one that's perfect, one that's acceptable and one that's completely wrong – from a woman's point of view. Answering the right way is simple – once you realise how women think – and you will be guaranteed to give the perfect answer every time.

Situation 1

You are invited to a cocktail party. Your partner has purchased a blue dress for this special occasion. She's standing in front of the mirror, holding up a pair of gold shoes in one hand and a pair of blue shoes in the other and says, 'Darling, which shoes should I wear with my new dress?'

a. You answer 'The gold ones.' Your partner asks indignantly, 'What's wrong with the blue ones? After all, I paid a fortune for them and you hate them, don't you?' And finally, she accuses you of not liking her style of clothing.

b. You compliment her on her dress, for example by saying, 'You look so breathtaking in the dress that you will get everyone's attention tonight. I'm such a lucky guy that you're going to the party with me.' If you really are a lucky guy, she will not ask again.

c. You just ask her in reply, 'Have you already chosen a pair, darling?' To this she will reply with slight uncertainty, 'The gold ones,' because she has already decided on them. To that you reply, 'Wow! Great choice! You'll look fabulous! I love them!'

Situation 2

You've just come home from the office and are having dinner with your partner. After she has asked you in great detail about your day (you were starting to feel like it was an interrogation), she starts telling you about her own day. She relates that on her way home she slipped on the pavement and broke the heel of her new high-heeled shoe.

a. You interrupt your partner and say: 'You know, you really shouldn't wear high heels when you go shopping. Why don't you wear flat shoes? That's safer.' Then she indignantly asks why you don't just listen when she tells you something.

b. You let her finish and then tell her that according to a study you've recently read, many accidents happen while wearing high-heeled shoes. She ignores this intentionally before continuing to tell you about the rest of her day.

c. You listen attentively and nod agreement now and then or mumble approvingly and ask, 'You haven't hurt yourself, darling, have you?' which she will deny with a smile before telling you more about her day.

Situation 3

Your partner phones you at work five minutes before the weekly meeting of the heads of department. She tells you irately that the rear tyre of her car was flat when she came back after shopping.

a. You interrupt her and say, 'How often do I tell you that you have to have the pressure checked regularly at the garage? If you had done it, this would never have happened.' She might then answer with a barrage of abuse and hang up on you.

b. You interrupt your partner carefully (reminding her of the meeting) and ask her to tell you the rest of the story in the evening when you have more time to listen to her.

c. You ask your secretary to tell the other participants of the meeting that you will be late because of an emergency – loud enough for your partner to hear it. You then take a few minutes to listen to her carefully and to comfort her.

Answer C was the perfect one every time and A was the answer your partner does not want to hear. The principle behind this is simple – women think aloud and consider it friendly because it lets them share their thoughts. They also like to get things off their chest in order to be able to cope better. Men often misunderstand this and think they are being given a list of problems to solve as soon as possible. Women don't expect answers to these questions (and definitely don't want suggestions or solutions) but prefer an attentive listener. Most of the time women know the answers and simply want affirmation.

Next are three more situations, similar to the ones above. Put your answer in the space below the situations. Then ask your partner to fill in which answer she would have wanted or expected from you. Now you can show her that you not only understand the problem, but are also ready to apply your knowledge.

Situation 4

Spring has arrived. It's time to mothball your winter clothes and get out your spring wear. Your partner has been doing that for the whole afternoon and is now standing in front of you in her favourite dress and asks: 'Do you think this outfit makes me look too big?'

Your answer: _____

_____

_____

What your partner would have wanted you to say: _____

_____

_____

_____

Situation 5

Your partner, who works for a small drugs manufacturer, tells you that she had an argument with a co-worker in distribution because of an outstanding order. She complains about how uncooperative the other worker is. She says: 'I almost came to blows with her. I really don't know what else I should do.'

Your answer: _____

_____

_____

What your partner would have wanted you to say: _____

_____

_____

_____

Situation 6

Your partner's sister has extravagant tastes and celebrates her birthday next weekend. Your partner has been thinking about a present for a long time and the evening before the party she shows you the gift she has selected, an ornate silver picture frame, and says, 'Do you think she'll like it? They also had plainer ones. Should I have purchased one of those instead?'

Your answer: _____

_____

_____

What your partner would have wanted you to say: _____

_____

_____

_____

# What's That Supposed to Mean? - The Enlightenment Test

Communication problems between men and women often arise because one doesn't understand what the other wants from them. The following test helps you find out how you communicate. Do you talk in plain English? Or do you express your wishes and opinions indirectly? Do you often exaggerate and lose yourself in details? Or are you more reserved and limit yourself to the essentials?

Find out now and learn how your partner communicates.

1. **Your boss asks you to obtain some information and gives you the phone number of a business partner who will help you with your research. You call him but he cannot help you after all. He gives you the phone number of somebody else who can. Unfortunately you cannot reach this second person. What do you do?**
    a) You explain the situation to your boss in great detail; how you have proceeded, who you've spoken to and what you will do next. After all, he has to be kept up to date. (Type C)
    b) You keep trying to contact the second person. You only call your boss when you get the information he needs – otherwise there's nothing to report. (Type A)
    c) If you still haven't been able to reach the contact person after two days, you give your boss a status report and tell him that you will keep following up. Otherwise he might think you had forgotten. (Type B)

2. **Your rich aunt turns 75 and you can't go to her party so you decide to send her a card. What kind of card do you choose?**
   a) You choose a card with a short poem or a pleasant saying inside so you don't have to write much yourself. (Type A)
   b) You choose a plain card and write a long, very personal text inside. If there's not enough room, you add a piece of paper inside. (Type C)
   c) You choose a card with a floral pattern, because you know that your aunt will like it, and write a few nice lines. (Type B)

3. **You're sitting in a comfortable chair and are reading a book when you have a sudden urge for a cup of coffee. However, you are too lazy to get up and make some and decide to ask your partner for it. What do you say?**
   a) 'Would you like a cup of coffee?' (Type C)
   b) 'Will you make a cup of coffee for me?' (Type A)
   c) 'I'd really love a cup of coffee right now, please.' (Type B)

4. **You've just come home from your company's Christmas party and your partner wants to know how it was. What's your reply?**
   a) You tell him about the most important events, like the manager's speech, the buffet, etc. but you are brief. (Type B)
   b) You say: 'Um... it was alright.' (Type A)
   c) You relate in great detail who was there, what kind of food you had, who you talked to and about what. You try not to forget anything or leave something out. (Type C)

5. **It's Saturday morning and you are having breakfast with your partner. You've planned a lot for today and have to do a number of things. How do you communicate this to your partner?**
   a) You give him the complete list in random order and mention all possibilities and outcomes. (Type C)
   b) After breakfast you say: 'I have to do a few things. See you later' and you leave. (Type A)
   c) You relate your plans briefly and try to co-ordinate your activities with his. (Type B)

6. **Somebody asks you: 'Can you change the oil in the car?' In your opinion, what do they mean?**
   a) The person wants to know whether you're able to change the oil. (Type A)
   b) The person is asking you to change the oil. (Type C)
   c) You're not sure and ask: 'Do you want to know whether I'm able to change the oil or do you want me to do it for you?' (Type B)

7. **You're with a group of friends and are having a lively discussion about various things. Often, several people are talking at the same time. How would you judge the course of the conversation?**
    a) Normal. After all, you often start talking about one thing yourself and suddenly change the topic, then return to the first issue a few minutes later. Anyway, you're chatting along with the others all the time. (Type C)
    b) Sometimes it gets a bit too loud for you, so you switch off or take time out. Also, you only take part in the conversation when you have to say something that's important. (Type B)
    c) After the third change of topic you are completely lost and don't have a clue what everyone else is talking about. You wish they'd stick to the point. And when everybody's talking at once, you can't think properly anyway. (Type A)

8. **You are on a driving trip with your partner and pass a pub. Your partner says: 'Would you like something to eat?' How do you respond?**
    a) You decline but ask in return whether she wants something. (Type B)
    b) You say, 'No thanks, not right now, and keep on driving because you are not hungry at the moment. (Type A)
    c) You are not hungry but reply, ,If you're hungry, we could just as well stop here., (Type C)

9. A couple are arguing and have the following conversation:
   Person A: 'You *never* agree with anything I say.'
   Person B: 'What do you mean *never*? I agreed with you this morning, I agreed with you last night and I agreed with you last Saturday so you can't say I *never* agree with you.'
   Person A: 'You say this *every time I bring it up*!'
   Person B: 'That's a lie! I don't say it every time!'
   Which of the statements could come from you?
   Those of person A (Type C)
   Those of person B (Type A)
   Neither (Type B)

10. Your partner comes back from a business trip where he tried to win over a new client. When you ask him how it went, he just says, 'Great. We got the assignment., What do you do?
    a) As everything's clear now, you are satisfied with the answer and are happy with his answer. (Type A)
    b) You are not satisfied with the answer and you keep asking until you get all the details you want. (Type C)
    c) You ask whether he wants to tell you in more detail, but are not disappointed if he declines. (Type B)

Evaluation: The Great Test of Communication

Compare your answers and check how often they are similar or identical. The more corresponding they are, the better your communication works. If, however, less than one third of your answers correspond, you need to be concerned about your relationship.

Evaluation: What's That Supposed to Mean? – The Enlightenment Test

Count how often you chose Type A, B or C. Each answer is one point. Read the section below for the type that scored most points.

Type A

You communicate like a man and display the features described in the introduction to this chapter.

Try to put yourself in your partner's position occasionally and take into account that women communicate in ways that are completely different from male communication.

A woman's brain is pre-wired for speech as a main form of expression and this is one of her strengths. With a greater flow of information between left and right hemisphere and more brain locations for speech than men, female talk is far more complex than that used by males. Women use words to show

participation, build relationships and as a form of reward. Women like to talk a lot and share their thoughts. If you take these aspects into account when talking to your partner and make a step in her direction by adapting to her way of communicating, you are on the way towards a happy relationship.

Type B

Depending on the situation, you communicate more like a man sometimes and more like a woman at others. This can be good, because by being flexible, you are able to adapt to the people you are talking with and can use the situation to your advantage. Obviously you have realised that communication is not only about what you mean and say, but also about considering how the other person might understand it. This takes some sensitivity and far-sightedness, but you seem to have enough of that, too.

Type C

You communicate like a woman and display the features described in the introduction to this chapter.

You need to put yourself in your partner's position and take into account that men communicate in a way that differs significantly from women, as described at the beginning of this chapter.

Most men cannot multi-track because the male brain is a mono-tracked system – it does 'one thing at a time'. Men can find their way from A to B via a maze of back streets, but are

not able to talk about more than one thing at a time. Men rarely show their sympathy or affection in words, but more by their actions, preferring to stay silent and not let others share their thoughts.

If you take all these points into account when talking with your partner, and take a step in his direction by adapting to his way of communicating, you are on the way to a happy relationship.

Do You Wish Your Partner Came With An Instruction Manual?

Then take a look at the wonderful series of relationship books by Barbara & Allan Pease

Why Men Don't Listen & Women Can't Read Maps

Explores the differences between men and women in the humorous style of writing we associate with Allan and Barbara Pease. This amazing book has sold more than 10 million copies worldwide!

Revealed in this book:
- Why men can only do one thing at a time
- Why women talk so much
- Why women need love, but men want sex
- Why men won't ask for directions
- How to get the opposite sex to do want you want them to do

www.peaseinternational.com

Why Men Lie & Women Cry

The sequel to the international bestseller *Why Men Don't Listen & Women Can't Read Maps.* Here the Pease's take lessons learned from the first book, and use them to explain common relationship problems.

Revealed in this book:
- Why men avoid commitment
- Why men everywhere feel women nag them
- Women's secret point scoring system
- Solving the seven biggest mysteries about the opposite sex

And the fabulous new MINI book ~

Why Men Can Only Do One Thing At A Time & Women Never Stop Talking

For anyone who has ever laid awake at night wondering why their partner just doesn't understand! The little book of sound advice from the world's foremost experts in relationships....

The perfect hardcover giftbook!

www.peaseinternational.com

HOT DVD's and CD's

The Best of Body Language

A 60 minute DVD or VHS showing the highlights of over 15 years of hilarious television, based on the No. 1 best-selling book. This programme uses hidden cameras, live audience participation and newsreel of various human miscommunication, including real fight scenes, business interviews and people telling real lies!

How To Develop Powerful Communication Skills ~ Managing The Differences Between Men & Women

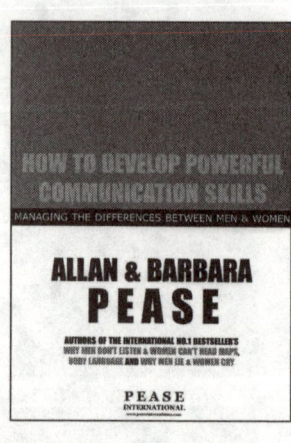

Containing a DVD and two CD's this programme shows -
- What men and women need to do to get on in business
- Why women read minds and men won't ask for directions
- The male boss; his female staff and the cold war
- How to avoid arguments, conflicts and disagreements
- Female Intuition; the walking radar detector
- How to persuade the opposite sex to say 'yes'

www.peaseinternational.com

How To Make Appointments By Telephone (CD Pack)

Your phone can create lots of cash!

This is an amazingly cost-effective, flexible and dynamic technique that will bring you spectacular results. This technique is used by many of the world's largest sales organisations and promises an average success rate of 7 out of 10 on cold calls. This is the most powerful appointments making tool you'll ever see!

Questions Are The Answers ~ CD or Cassette

Top level networkers are not 'natural' or 'born'. Top level networking is a skill - a learnable skill, and Questions are the Answers, gives you the techniques and shows you how to use them, how to measure and improve your progress and what to observe when dealing with people.

Now available to Direct Selling Groups around the world is some of the best training and development products ever including the best selling audio Questions are the Answers. This is THE sales programme to own and comes with a double sided laminated "Priorities Card".

GET YOURS TODAY!

www.peaseinternational.com

BUSINESS BOOKS

The Definitive Book of Body Language

This brand new book isolates, examines and explains in simple terms, each component of body language. Regardless of your vocation or position in life, you will be able to use it to obtain a better understanding of life's most complex event – a face-to-face encounter with another person. It will make you more aware of your own non-verbal cues and signals, and will show you how to use them to communicate effectively and how to get the reactions you want.

Write Language

Both in your business and your personal life, you'll discover that **WRITE LANGUAGE** is a unique and powerful book. It's a superb investment.

This books shows you amongst other things –
· How to persuade your readers to do what you want them to do
· How to get immediate attention from your reader
· How to make money through direct mail letters

No matter how many letters you write, this book will help you communicate more effectively.

www.peaseinternational.com

Talk Language

Some people are so busy 'communicating' that they don't listen to each other. *Talk Language* tells you how to understand what people are *really* saying, and why. It shows you how to decode a wide range of everyday signals, so you can get the message or intentions a speaker is really conveying – whether intentionally or not.

Talk Language will help you to express yourself clearly and concisely. Its message can be applied to almost every facet of everyday life. You'll learn
- How to ask powerful questions
- How to make intelligent buying decisions
- How to resist being manipulated
- How to sound interesting and appealing

Questions Are The Answers

The Direct Marketing Business has evolved virtually overnight without fanfare or advertising and could eventually become the largest business system of them all. Its success has been based on the referral-based distribution system and is driven almost entirely by the enthusiasm of its members. It is one of the most dynamic opportunities ever created by the mind of man, and Allan Pease has given everyone the key to unlock this system.

This is THE sales book to own

www.peaseinternational.com

Why not use Allan Pease as guest speaker for your next conference or seminar?

Pease International (Australia) Pty Ltd
Pease International (UK) Ltd

P.O. Box 1260
Buderim 4556
Queensland
AUSTRALIA
Tel: ++61 7 5445 5600
Fax: ++61 7 5445 5688

Liberty House
16 Newbold Terrace
Leamington Spa CV 32 4 EG
UNITED KINGDOM
Tel: ++44 (0)1926 889900
Fax: ++44 (0)1926 421100

email: (Aust) info@peaseinternational.com
 (UK) ukoffice@peaseinternational.com
website: www.peaseinternational.com

Also by Allan Pease:

Video Programs
 Body Language Series
 Silent Signals
 The Interview
 How to Make Appointments by Telephone

DVD Programs
 The Best of Body Language
 How to Develop Powerful Communication—Managing the Differences Between Men and Women

Audio Programs
 The Four Personality Styles
 How to Make Appointments by Telephone
 How to Remember Names, Faces & Lists
 Why Men Don't Listen and Women Can't Read Maps
 Questions are the Answers

Books
 The Definitive Book Of Body Language
 Why Men Don't Listen & Women Can't Read Maps
 Why Men Lie & Women Cry
 Why Men Can Only Do One Thing At A Time & Women Never Stop Talking
 How Compatible Are You?
 Talk Language
 Write Language
 Questions Are The Answers
 The Bumper Book of Rude & Politically Incorrect Jokes
 Politically Incorrect Jokes Men Love